easy party food

easy party food

simply delicious recipes for your perfect party

RYLAND
PETERS
& SMALL

LONDON NEW YORK

Senior Designer Sonya Nathoo
Editor Rebecca Woods
Picture Research Emily Westlake
Production Toby Marshall
Art Director Leslie Harrington
Publishing Director Alison Starling

Indexer Hilary Bird

First published in 2011
by Ryland Peters & Small
20–21 Jockey's Fields
London WC1R 4BW
and
Ryland Peters & Small, Inc.
519 Broadway, 5th Floor
New York, NY10012

www.rylandpeters.com

10 9 8 7 6 5 4 3 2 1

Text © Fiona Beckett, Julz Beresford,
Susannah Blake, Maxine Clark, Ross
Dobson, Clare Ferguson, Lydia France,
Jennifer Joyce, Caroline Marson, Annie
Nichols, Isidora Popovic, Annie Rigg,
Jennie Shapter, Fran Warde and
Ryland Peters & Small 2011

Design and photographs
© Ryland Peters & Small 2011

UK ISBN 978 1 84975 161 2
US ISBN 978 1 84975 162 9

A catalogue record for this book is
available from the British Library.

Library of Congress Cataloging-in-
Publication Data

Easy party food : simply delicious
recipes for your perfect party.
       p. cm.
  Includes index.
  ISBN 978-1-84975-162-9
  1. Entertaining. 2. Cooking. I.
Ryland Peters & Small.
  TX731.E23 2011
  642'.4--dc23
                              2011013337

Printed in China

Notes
• All spoon measurements are level,
unless otherwise specified.

• Weights and measurements have
been rounded up or down slightly
to make measuring easier.

• Ovens should be preheated to the
specified temperature. Recipes in this
book were tested using a regular oven.
If using a fan-assisted oven, follow
the manufacturer's instructions for
adjusting temperatures.

• When a recipe calls for the grated
zest of citrus fruit, buy unwaxed fruit
and wash well before using. If you
can only find treated fruit, scrub well
in warm soapy water and rinse before
using.

contents

introduction

Great party food should be about picking the best seasonal ingredients and preparing and presenting dishes with imagination, care and a real sense of festivity. But, that's not to say that preparing food for a large gathering should be difficult or stressful. We arrange parties to bring together the people we love. No-one wants to be sweating over a hot stove while our friends and family laugh and chat around us. *Easy Party Food* is full of achievable yet impressive looking dishes from recipes that are designed to be simple to follow, so you can spend more time enjoying yourself.

Party food has also grown up in recent years. It is no longer customary to be served soggy sandwiches, limp celery sticks and bowls of processed store-bought snacks. Instead, many of the recipes in this book take their inspiration from cuisines around the world. Platters of Moroccan-inspired dips are circulated with spicy Cajun nuts and little French tartlets; on the buffet table, a classic lasagne may sit alongside a Thai beef salad. But there is still room for some revamped classic dishes – the retro prawn cocktail is given a modern make-over with shot glasses, and of course, it wouldn't be a party without a big plate of sausage rolls or marinaded chicken wings.

Whatever your taste, or whatever the occasion, *Easy Party Food* will inspire you to try out some new recipes when entertaining so you can enjoy the experience of seeing your guests' eyes light up, their eager fingers seizing the tasty morsels on display and then offering their heartfelt gratitude to you for hosting a wonderful party. For a little guidance, just follow the basic guidelines, opposite, and, most importantly of all, enjoy yourself.

Calculate how much food you will need – for a typical drinks party, you'll want to provide an average of eight different canapé choices and allow about two of each per person. Don't forget to check if any of your guests have any food allergies or specific dietary requirements.

Check your equipment as it's rare to have enough glasses, serving platters, napkins or ice to cater for a crowd, so make sure that you buy, hire or borrow enough for your purposes before the event.

Get ahead on the food preparation by drawing up a detailed shopping list and find out where to source any more unusual ingredients in advance. Wherever possible, make a few of your chosen canapés (or elements of, such as tartlet cases) in advance and refrigerate or freeze them until needed.

Match the occasion and the food to the time of year – seasonal food is much more inviting – light, fresh food in the warmth of summer and comforting food when it's miserable and cold.

Presentation can make a party memorable, so make the food look eye-catching, dramatic and appetizing. Invest in complementary serving dishes and be artistic in arranging the food itself, using garnishes and decorations.

Food hygiene and safety is crucial when you are catering for a party. Check use-by dates, keep surfaces and equipment clean, store cooked and raw foods separately, keep food covered until needed and wash hands frequently.

light bites & dips

spicy cajun mixed nuts

155 g/5½ oz. unsalted cashews

155 g/5½ oz. pecans

140 g/5 oz. pistachios

1 teaspoon cayenne pepper

1 teaspoon smoked paprika (pimentón)

½ teaspoon dried thyme

1 teaspoon fine sea salt

1 tablespoon soft brown sugar

1 tablespoon olive oil

a baking sheet lined with baking parchment

serves 10–12

Cashews, pecans and pistachio nuts are given in the ingredient list here, but feel free to choose your favourite nuts for this. Buy the nuts in bulk and you will save lots of money. And besides, this is a recipe you will want to make more than once. It's a good nibble to offer if you are planning to serve a more spicy meal later on.

Preheat the oven to 180°C (350°F) Gas 4.

Put all of the nuts in a large bowl. Add the cayenne pepper, paprika, thyme, salt and sugar and mix to combine. Stir in the olive oil. Tip the nuts out onto the prepared baking sheet, spreading them out into a single layer.

Bake in the preheated oven for 10 minutes, stirring about halfway through the cooking time. Let cool completely on the baking sheet before spooning into serving bowls. These nuts will keep in an airtight container for 7–10 days.

cheese balls

2 tablespoons plain/
all-purpose flour

2 tablespoons milk

½ teaspoon smoked
sweet paprika (*pimentón
dulce*)

1 egg

1 garlic clove, crushed

150 g/5½ oz. Manchego
cheese, finely grated

150 g/5½ oz. goats'
cheese, preferably
Spanish, crumbled

2 egg whites

1 teaspoon chopped
fresh thyme leaves

1 tablespoon finely
chopped Serrano ham
or prosciutto

sea salt and freshly
ground white pepper

oil, for frying

an electric deep-fat fryer

cocktail sticks/toothpicks

serves 4

Manchego cheese is popular all over Spain. It is to
the Spanish what Parmesan is to the Italians. The mix
of Manchego sheep's cheese and Spanish goats' cheese
balances each other perfectly. A treat for your guests.

Put the flour and milk in a bowl and stir until smooth. Add the
paprika, salt, pepper and the whole egg. Add the garlic and both
cheeses and mix well.

Put the egg whites in a bowl and whisk until stiff. Fold one-third into
the flour mixture and mix well, then gently fold in the remaining egg
whites making sure not to lose all the air. Sprinkle with the fresh
thyme and ham.

Fill a deep-fat fryer with oil to the manufacturer's recommended
level and heat the oil to 195°C (380°F). Using a teaspoon, run the
spoon through the mixture collecting an even amount of thyme and
ham and drop a heaped spoonful into the hot oil. Cook the mixture
for 3 minutes or until the cheese ball is golden brown (you may have
to do this in batches). Drain on kitchen paper and serve immediately
with cocktail sticks/toothpicks.

potato skins with green dip

12 large baking potatoes

200 ml/¾ cup olive oil

400 g/14 oz. mature Cheddar cheese, grated

green dip

400 ml/1⅔ cups sour cream

2 bunches of fresh chives, chopped

2 bunches of spring onions/scallions, chopped

a bunch of fresh flat leaf parsley, chopped

sea salt and freshly ground black pepper

a baking sheet, lightly oiled

serves 24

These crunchy golden, potato skins are delicious with a fresh green dip, and the soft potato middles can be saved for making mashed potatoes.

Preheat the oven to 180°C (350°F) Gas 4.

Using a small, sharp knife, pierce each potato right through the middle. Bake in the preheated oven for 1 hour 10 minutes or until cooked through. Remove and set aside until cool enough to handle. Cut each potato in half lengthways and scoop out the soft middles, leaving a thin layer lining the skin. Cut each skin half into 4 wedges, then cover and refrigerate until needed.

To make the dip, put the sour cream, chives, spring onions/scallions and parsley in a bowl. Add salt and pepper to taste and mix well.

Adjust the oven temperature to 220°C (425°F) Gas 7. Brush oil over the potato skins and arrange in a single layer on the oiled baking sheet. Bake at the top of the oven for 30 minutes until golden, moving the potato skins around occasionally so they cook evenly. Remove from the oven and reduce the heat to 200°C (400°F) Gas 6.

Sprinkle the potato skins with cheese and return to the oven for 5–10 minutes, until the cheese is melted or crunchy, checking after 5 minutes if you want it melted. Serve with the green dip.

2 large ripe avocados

freshly squeezed juice of 2 limes

1 small green chilli, deseeded and finely chopped

4 spring onions/scallions, very finely chopped

1 ripe medium tomato, skinned, deseeded and coarsely chopped

2–3 tablespoons coarsely chopped fresh coriander/cilantro

sea salt and freshly ground black pepper

tortilla chips or crudités, to serve

serves 4

the best guacamole with tortilla chips

Use only perfectly ripe avocados for this – overripe ones will make the guacamole discolour quickly. To make it go further for larger numbers, stir in 150 ml/⅔ cup sour cream – it will now serve 6–8 as a dip. Just double the quantities to serve more.

Halve the avocados, remove the stones and scoop out the flesh into a bowl. Mash with a fork to give a coarse texture. Mix in half the lime juice, the chilli, spring onions/scallions, chopped tomato and coriander/cilantro.

Taste and season with salt, pepper and more lime juice if necessary. Don't make this too far in advance because it will discolour quickly. Cover tightly with clingfilm/plastic wrap, then stir well before serving. Serve with tortilla chips or crudités.

harissa hoummus with pomegranate vinaigrette

500 g/1 lb 2 oz. dried chickpeas, soaked in water overnight

8 tablespoons tahini

2 teaspoons harissa paste

6 garlic cloves

grated zest of 2 unwaxed lemons and freshly squeezed juice of 4

sea salt

pomegranate vinaigrette

seeds from 1 pomegranate

2 tablespoons dark honey

2 big handfuls fresh flat leaf parsley, chopped

8–10 tablespoons extra virgin olive oil

sea salt, to taste

3 tablespoons toasted sesame seeds, to serve

serves 20

Homemade hoummus is quite a different beast from its supermarket equivalent – much bigger on both flavour and texture. This version is big on looks too. Serve at room temperature with toasts and flatbreads.

Put the drained chickpeas in a pan of fresh, unsalted, cold water. Bring to the boil and cook for 1½ hours until soft. Drain, reserving the cooking water, and reserve 50 g/2 oz. of the chickpeas to serve.

In a food processor, blend the remaining chickpeas and all the other ingredients, except the salt, to a soft purée, adding a little of the cooking water at a time until you have a smooth paste. Taste and season with salt. Transfer to a large shallow bowl.

Gently combine all the pomegranate vinaigrette ingredients in a bowl and add the reserved chickpeas. Spoon this mixture onto the hoummus. Scatter the toasted sesame seeds over the top to serve.

crumbled cheese dip with herbs and pomegranate seeds

300 g/10½ oz. feta cheese, crumbled

freshly squeezed juice of 1 lemon

5 tablespoons extra-virgin olive oil

a pinch of red chilli/hot red pepper flakes, crushed

1 small red onion, finely diced

1 tablespoon each finely chopped fresh parsley, dill and mint

2 tablespoons pomegranate molasses

4 tablespoons pomegranate seeds

flatbread, warmed, to serve

makes 350 ml/1½ cups

This middle-eastern inspired dip is great served on a platter with slices of warmed flatbread, or as part of a meze or buffet selection. The creamy cheese goes wonderfully with a tangy bite of pomegranate seeds.

Arrange the crumbled cheese in a serving bowl. Pour the lemon juice and olive oil over it. Sprinkle the chilli/hot red pepper flakes, onion and herbs on top. Drizzle with the pomegranate molasses and sprinkle with the pomegranate seeds to finish. Serve with plenty of flatbread for dipping.

kipfler crisps with sour cream and caviar dip

800 g/1 lb 12 oz. Kipfler
potatoes (about 8) or
other small waxy potato

125 ml/½ cup olive oil

125 ml/½ cup vegetable
oil

250 ml/1 cup sour cream
or crème fraîche

1 tablespoon snipped
fresh chives

2–3 tablespoons caviar
or salmon roe

sea salt flakes, to sprinkle

serves 6–8

This recipe takes the humble potato to new heights. Gourmet crisps/chips are made using firm, waxy potatoes which gives them a lovely golden colour and buttery flavour. They are good enough to enjoy on their own but a real treat served this way. You don't have to buy expensive caviar – salmon pearls (roe) are also ideal; it's the salty flavour burst followed by the creamy indulgence of sour cream that's delicious.

Cut the potatoes into slices about 2–3 mm/⅛ inch thick. Bring a large saucepan of lightly salted water to the boil. Add the potatoes, cover the pan and remove from the heat. Leave in the hot water for 5 minutes. Drain well and arrange the potatoes on a wire rack in a single layer until completely cool.

Put the oils in a saucepan or large frying pan/skillet set over high heat. When the oil is hot, cook the potato slices in batches for 5–6 minutes each, turning once or twice, until crisp and golden. Remove from the oil using a metal slotted spoon and drain on kitchen paper.

Put the crisps/chips in a bowl, sprinkle liberally with sea salt flakes and toss to coat. Combine the sour cream or crème fraîche and chives in a small bowl, top with the caviar and serve with the crisps/chips on the side for dipping.

polenta chips with green Tabasco mayonnaise

1 litre/4 cups chicken or vegetable stock

250 g/1½ cups instant polenta

2 tablespoons butter

50 g/1¾ oz. Parmesan cheese, finely grated

250 ml/1 cup vegetable oil

125 ml/½ cup light olive oil

30 g/3 tablespoons plain/all-purpose flour

125 ml/½ cup mayonnaise

2 teaspoons green Tabasco sauce

2 baking sheets, lightly oiled

makes about 60

Don't we all just love something fried every now and then? Everything in moderation. Although, be warned that it is hard to stop at just one!

Put the stock in a saucepan and bring to the boil. While the stock is boiling, pour in the polenta in a steady stream and whisk until it is all incorporated. Continue whisking for about 2 minutes, until the mixture is smooth and thickened. Remove from the heat and stir through the butter and Parmesan until well combined. Spoon half of the mixture into each of the baking sheets. Use the back of a metal spoon to smooth the top. Cover and refrigerate for at least 4 hours, until firm.

Transfer the polenta to a chopping board. Trim the edges. Cut the block lengthways in half – then cut into 1-cm/½-inch thick slices, to make about 60 chips.

Pour the oils into a frying pan/skillet and heat over medium/high heat. The oil is ready if a small piece of the polenta mixture sizzles on contact. Put about one quarter of the chips in a colander and sprinkle over some of the flour. Shake the colander to coat the chips in the flour and to remove the excess. Add these to the oil and cook for 4–5 minutes, turning often, until golden. Transfer the cooked chips to some kitchen paper to absorb the excess oil. Cover with foil and keep warm in a low oven while you cook the second batch. Repeat with the other chips.

Combine the mayonnaise and Tabasco in a bowl to serve alongside the hot chips as a dip.

roasted red pepper and walnut dip

This is a traditional Syrian dip called muhammara. There it would be served as part of a meze selection, with hoummus, baba ganoush, pickles, olives, cheese and flatbreads. It's perfect for entertaining as it benefits from being made a day in advance.

3 large red bell peppers

1 slice of day-old sourdough bread, cut into small pieces

100 g/3½ oz. walnut halves, coarsely chopped

½ teaspoon dried chilli/hot red pepper flakes

1 tablespoon sun-dried tomato paste

2 garlic cloves, chopped

2 teaspoons freshly squeezed lemon juice

1 tablespoon balsamic vinegar

2 teaspoons sugar

1 teaspoon ground cumin

2 tablespoons olive oil, plus extra to serve

chopped pistachios, to sprinkle

sea salt and freshly ground black pepper

toasted flatbread, roughly torn, to serve

serves 6–8

Cook the bell peppers one at a time by skewering each one on a fork and holding it directly over a gas flame for 10–15 minutes, until the skin is blackened all over. Alternatively, put them on a baking sheet and then in an oven preheated to 220°C (425°F) Gas 7. Cook them for about 10–15 minutes, until the skin has puffed up and blackened all over. Transfer to a bowl, cover with a dish towel and leave until cool enough to handle.

Using your hands, remove the skin and seeds from the bell peppers and tear the flesh into pieces. (Avoid rinsing with water, as this will remove the smoky flavour.) Put it in a food processor and add the remaining ingredients. Process to a coarse paste. Season to taste with salt and pepper and transfer to a bowl. Cover with clingfilm/plastic wrap and refrigerate for 8 hours or ideally overnight to allow the flavours to fully develop.

To serve, bring the dip to room temperature and transfer it to a shallow bowl. Drizzle with olive oil and sprinkle with chopped pistachios. Serve with torn toasted flatbreads. It will keep in an airtight container in the refrigerator for 4–5 days.

roasted aubergine and caper dip

This rich, smoky-tasting dip makes a perfect companion to the Roasted Red Pepper and Walnut Dip on page 27. Whet your guests' appetites by circulating them on a platter with plenty of bread to enjoy with drinks.

Preheat the oven to 180°C (350°F) Gas 4.

Put the onion in a small bowl and pour in the lemon juice. Set aside. Prick the aubergines/eggplant all over with a fork and put them directly on the oven shelf. Roast them in the preheated oven for just under 1 hour, turning them over occasionally. When cool enough to handle, carefully peel off the blackened skin and discard it along with the stalks. Chop the flesh and put it in a large bowl. Add the onion, tomatoes, garlic, capers, spring onion/scallion, olive oil and parsley. Season with salt and pepper and mix well. Serve with toasted pita bread or flatbread for dipping.

1 small red onion, finely chopped

freshly squeezed juice of 1 lemon

2 large aubergines/eggplant

2 ripe plum tomatoes, peeled and diced

1 garlic clove, finely chopped

1 teaspoon small capers

1 spring onion/scallion, chopped

4 tablespoons olive oil

2 tablespoons finely chopped flat leaf parsley

sea salt and freshly ground black pepper

toasted pita bread or flatbread, to serve

serves 4–6

2 tablespoons sunflower or safflower oil

2 medium carrots, cut into matchsticks

50 g/½ cup mangetout/snow peas, cut into matchsticks

50 g/¾ cup shiitake mushrooms, chopped

2.5-cm/1-inch piece fresh ginger, peeled and grated

1 small red chilli, deseeded and chopped

50 g/1 cup beansprouts

2 spring onions/scallions, thinly sliced

1 tablespoon light soy sauce

2 teaspoons plain/all-purpose flour

20 x 20-cm/8 x 8-inch square spring-roll wrappers

oil for deep-frying

chilli dipping sauce

5 tablespoons sweet chilli sauce

1 tablespoon light soy sauce

a deep-fat fryer

makes 16

mini spring rolls with chilli dipping sauce

Spring rolls are best served immediately after cooking, but to keep last-minute preparation minimal make the filling up to 24 hours ahead. Fill the spring roll wrappers about an hour before cooking, but keep them covered so they remain moist until cooked.

Heat the sunflower/safflower oil in a wok or frying pan/skillet and stir-fry the carrots, mangetout/snow peas, mushrooms and ginger for 1 minute. Add the chilli, beansprouts and spring onions/scallions and stir-fry for 1–2 minutes, or until the vegetables are tender-crisp. Remove from the heat, stir in the soy sauce and set aside to cool.

Next, make the chilli dipping sauce. Mix together the sweet chilli sauce and soy sauce in a small bowl and transfer to a serving dish.

In a small bowl, mix the flour with 1 tablespoon water to make a paste. Cut the spring-roll wrappers in half diagonally and place under a damp cloth to keep moist. Remove one at a time to fill.

Divide the filling into four and put a quarter of one batch on the long cut side of a wrapper, placing it along the centre, slightly in from the edge. Fold over the side flaps. Brush a little flour paste on the pointed end of the wrapper and roll up towards the point, pressing the end to seal. Repeat with the remaining wrappers. Keep covered until ready to cook.

Fill a deep-fat fryer with oil to the manufacturer's recommended level. Heat the oil to 180°C (350°F) and deep-fry the rolls in batches for 2–3 minutes, until crisp and golden. Drain on kitchen paper. Serve hot with the chilli dipping sauce.

125 g/4½ oz. crab meat

50 g/2 oz. cooked and shelled prawns/shrimp, chopped

4 canned water chestnuts, finely chopped

2 spring onions/scallions, finely chopped

2.5-cm/1-inch piece fresh ginger, peeled and grated

1 small chilli, deseeded and finely chopped

1 tablespoon fresh coriander/cilantro, chopped

1 tablespoon light soy sauce

20 x 8–9-cm/3½-inch round wonton wrappers

toasted sesame seeds, to sprinkle

soy and ginger dipping sauce

3 tablespoons light soy sauce

3 tablespoons Chinese rice wine or dry sherry

1-cm/½-inch piece fresh ginger, peeled and sliced

a steamer

makes 20

crab wonton wraps with dipping sauce

These bite-sized morsels are typical of Chinese dim sum – they look elegant, smell tantalizing and taste good! Use fresh crab meat for the very best flavour. If you do need to use frozen crab meat, make sure it is well drained before using.

In a bowl mix together the crab meat, prawns/shrimp, water chestnuts, spring onions/scallions, ginger, chilli, coriander/cilantro and soy sauce.

Brush the edges of a wonton wrapper with water. Place a heaped teaspoon of filling in the centre. Draw up the edges and press together firmly. Repeat to make 20 wonton wraps. Cover and refrigerate until ready to cook.

In a small bowl, combine the dipping sauce ingredients.

Put a layer of parchment paper in the base of a steamer and arrange the wonton wraps in the steamer, making sure they do not touch each other. Place over a pan of boiling water, cover and steam for 5 minutes. Cook in batches if necessary.

Sprinkle with toasted sesame seeds and serve with the soy and ginger dipping sauce.

chilli salt squid

400 g/14 oz. cleaned squid (1 large tube)

2 tablespoons cornflour/cornstarch

1 tablespoon plain/all-purpose flour

½ teaspoon ground white pepper

½ teaspoon mild chilli powder

3 teaspoons sea salt

1 large red chilli, thinly sliced

a small handful of fresh coriander/cilantro leaves, chopped

vegetable oil, for deep-frying

lemon wedges, to serve

serves 4

We really ought to eat more squid; it is cheap and in plentiful supply and, when served with small forks or cocktail sticks, is a great party bite for guests to pick at. Fresh squid can look a little scary, but it really is superior to the frozen stuff. It should be cooked in one of two ways: very quickly or for a long time – anywhere in between makes it tough.

Cut the squid tube down one side so that it opens up. Use a sharp knife to trim and discard any internal membranes. Cut it lengthways into 2-cm/1-inch wide strips, then cut each strip in half. Combine the flours, white pepper, chilli powder and salt in a large bowl. Half-fill a saucepan with the vegetable oil and heat over high heat until the surface of the oil shimmers.

Toss half of the squid pieces in the flour mixture, quickly shaking off the excess, and add them to the oil. Cook for about 2 minutes, until deep golden. Remove with a slotted spoon and drain on kitchen paper. Repeat with the remaining squid. Add the chilli slices to the oil and cook for just a few seconds. Remove from the pan and drain on kitchen paper. Put the squid and chilli on a serving plate and sprinkle with the coriander/cilantro. Serve while still warm with plenty of lemon wedges on the side for squeezing.

1 tablespoon olive oil

300 g/10½ oz. small, spicy fresh chorizo sausages, cut into 1-cm/½-inch slices

100 ml/scant ½ cup red wine

crusty bread, to serve

serves 4

chorizo in red wine

Chorizo comes in many different varieties. You can get smoked, unsmoked, fresh and cured. For this recipe spicy chorizo, the size of regular breakfast sausages, is ideal. Large quantities of paprika give rich colour and pungent flavour. Serve with cocktail sticks/toothpicks or small forks for picking and pieces of crusty bread to mop up the juices.

Put the oil in a heavy-based frying pan/skillet and heat until smoking. Add the chorizo and cook for 1 minute. Reduce the heat, add the wine and cook for 5 minutes. Transfer to a serving dish and set aside to develop the flavours. Serve warm.

sausage rolls

375 g/13 oz. ready-rolled
**puff pastry, thawed if
frozen**

**1 tablespoon Dijon
mustard**

24 cocktail sausages

1 egg, lightly beaten

a baking sheet, lined with
baking parchment

makes 24

No party is complete without a heaped dish of hot
bite-sized sausage rolls. All you need to add is a bowl
of ketchup to serve with them.

Preheat the oven to 190°C (375°F) Gas 5.

Sprinkle a little flour on a clean work surface. Unroll the pastry, and
if it's thicker than 2 mm/⅛ inch use a rolling pin to make it the right
thickness. Spread the mustard over the pastry.

With the long side of the pastry nearest you, cut the pastry vertically
into 6 equal strips. Cut each strip into 4. Place a sausage on each
piece of pastry and roll the pastry around it. Arrange on the prepared
baking sheet.

Score 2 or 3 small cuts in the top of each sausage roll with a sharp
knife and brush with the beaten egg.

Bake on the middle shelf of the preheated oven for 30 minutes,
or until golden.

sesame maple turkey fingers

4 tablespoons maple syrup, plus 3 tablespoons extra for dipping

1 small fresh red chilli, halved, deseeded and finely chopped

1 teaspoon sea salt

1 garlic clove, crushed

500 g/1 lb 2 oz. lean turkey breast

100 g/3½ oz. sesame seeds, lightly toasted

fresh mint leaves, to garnish

2 baking sheets

makes about 40

The maple syrup will only subtly flavour the turkey, so offer more in a bowl as a dipping sauce. If you're entertaining children, omit the chilli and garlic from the recipe and they will love the turkey fingers.

Put the maple syrup, half the chilli, the salt and garlic in a bowl and leave for 30 minutes.

Preheat the oven to 200°C (400°F) Gas 6.

Cut the turkey breast into strips (about 40 in total). Coat the turkey fingers with the maple syrup mixture, then with the sesame seeds. Arrange slightly apart on baking sheets and cook for about 8 minutes, until cooked through.

Put the remaining chilli and 3 tablespoons maple syrup in a small bowl as a dipping sauce. Scatter the mint leaves over and serve.

2 tablespoons olive oil

grated zest and freshly squeezed juice of 1 lemon

1 teaspoon balsamic vinegar

2 teaspoons chopped fresh thyme

225 g/8 oz. halloumi cheese, cut into 12 slices

1 large yellow bell pepper, halved lengthways

2 large red bell peppers, halved lengthways

freshly ground black pepper

salsa verde

3 tablespoons olive oil

1 garlic clove, finely chopped

5-cm/2-inch piece cucumber, deseeded and finely chopped

grated zest and freshly squeezed juice of 1 lime

2 tablespoons chopped fresh flat leaf parsley

2 tablespoons chopped fresh basil

1 teaspoon capers, rinsed and chopped

1 green chilli, finely chopped (optional)

cocktail sticks/toothpicks

makes 12

halloumi and pepper wraps with salsa verde

Halloumi is a Greek cheese which is fairly bland so lends itself to marinating with Mediterranean herbs before wrapping with pieces of char-grilled pepper. Make sure these are served hot while the cheese is soft as halloumi can become rubbery once cooled.

Preheat the grill/broiler to medium.

Mix the olive oil, lemon zest and juice, balsamic vinegar, thyme and black pepper together in a shallow dish. Add the slices of halloumi and set aside to marinate while preparing the peppers.

Put the peppers on the grill/broiler rack, skin-side up, and cook until they begin to soften and char. Do not overcook as they will be cooked again after wrapping. Place in a large bowl, cover and leave for 15 minutes. Meanwhile, mix the salsa verde ingredients together, adding the chilli if wished, and set aside to infuse.

Peel the skins off the peppers and remove the stalks and cores. Cut in half lengthways. Put a slice of halloumi in the centre of each pepper strip, allowing the cheese to protrude slightly over the edges of the pepper. Wrap the pepper over the cheese and secure with a cocktail stick/toothpick. Put on a shallow baking sheet and brush with the remaining marinade.

Cook under a preheated medium-high grill/broiler for 4–5 minutes on each side, or until the cheese softens and starts to brown and the peppers start to char. Serve drizzled with a little salsa verde.

rosemary mayonnaise

3 egg yolks

3 tablespoons fresh rosemary leaves

1 teaspoon Dijon mustard

3 tablespoons cider vinegar

500 ml/2 cups grapeseed oil

spice-rubbed potatoes

750 g/1 lb 10 oz. pink-skinned new potatoes, halved lengthways

1 teaspoon cayenne pepper

1 teaspoon caraway seeds

1 teaspoon coriander seeds

a small piece of cinnamon stick

1 garlic clove, crushed

1 teaspoon sea salt

2 tablespoons olive oil

a baking sheet

makes 50

warm spice-rubbed potatoes with rosemary mayonnaise

This recipe uses pink-skinned new potatoes for their charming colour and firm texture. If they're not available, you can substitute any large potatoes, peeled and cut to your preferred size.

For the mayonnaise, put all the ingredients, except the grapeseed oil, in a food processor and blend. With the motor running, slowly add the oil in droplets until the mayonnaise starts to thicken. Continue with an even trickle until you have incorporated all the oil. Spoon into a bowl and chill.

Cook the potatoes in a large pan of boiling water for about 12–15 minutes, until almost cooked. Drain and pat dry. Gently warm the spices in a small pan for about 2 minutes until their scent starts to pervade the kitchen. Put the warmed spices, garlic and salt in the clean food processor and blend to make a rough spice mix.

Preheat the oven to 200°C (400°F) Gas 6. Put the potatoes in a bowl with the olive oil and toss together. Using clean hands, rub the spice mixture onto the potatoes and bake them on a baking sheet in the preheated oven for about 20 minutes until golden. Serve with a generous dollop of rosemary mayonnaise.

tartlets & toasts

375 g/13 oz. ready-made shortcrust pastry

slow-roasted tomatoes

12–15 large ripe cherry tomatoes

2 finely chopped garlic cloves

1 tablespoon dried oregano

4 tablespoons olive oil

sea salt and freshly ground black pepper

herby cheese filling

80 g/3 oz. full-fat soft cheese with garlic and herbs (such as Boursin)

1 large egg, beaten

150 ml/⅔ cup double/heavy cream

4 tablespoons chopped fresh mixed herbs (such as parsley, basil, marjoram or chives)

75 g/2½ oz. feta cheese

tiny sprigs of thyme or cut chives, to finish

sea salt and freshly ground black pepper

a plain cookie cutter, 6 cm/2½ inch diameter

2 x 12-hole mini muffin tins

foil or baking parchment and baking beans

makes 24

slow-roasted tomato and herb tartlets with feta

Tiny tartlets are great to serve at a drinks party. They look stunning and have a secret pocket of feta cheese hiding in the herby filling underneath the tomatoes.

Preheat the oven to 200°C (400°F) Gas 6.

Roll out the pastry as thinly as possible on a lightly floured work surface. Use the cookie cutter to stamp out 24 circles. Line the muffin tin holes with the pastry circles, then prick the bases and chill or freeze for 15 minutes.

To blind bake the cases, line them with foil or parchment paper (flicking the edges inwards so that they don't catch on the dough), then fill with baking beans. Bake them in the centre of the oven for 10–12 minutes. Remove the foil or parchment and the beans and return them to the oven for 5–7 minutes to dry out completely.

Turn the oven down to 160°C (325°F) Gas 3. Cut the tomatoes in half around the middle. Arrange cut side up on a baking sheet. Put the chopped garlic, oregano, olive oil and lots of ground pepper into a bowl and mix well, then spoon or brush over the cut tomatoes. Bake slowly in the oven for about 1½–2 hours, checking every now and then. They should be slightly shrunk and still a brilliant red colour – if too dark, they will taste bitter.

Put the soft cheese into a bowl, add the egg, cream and chopped herbs and beat until smooth. Season well. Cut the feta into 24 small cubes that will fit inside the pastry cases.

When ready to bake, set the cases on a baking sheet, put a cube of feta in each one and top up with the garlic and herb mixture. Bake in the preheated oven at 180°C (350°F) Gas 4 for about 15–20 minutes or until the filling is set. Top each with a tomato half, a sprinkle of the cooking juices and a thyme sprig or chive stem. Serve warm.

13 slices fresh white bread

3 tablespoons olive oil, shaken with 1 crushed garlic clove and 1 teaspoon sea salt

100 g/3½ oz. anchovy fillets, chopped quite finely

1 garlic clove, crushed

1 tablespoon chopped fresh dill

1 tablespoon chopped fresh mint

200 g/7 oz. Little Gem or Boston lettuce, finely shredded

grated zest and freshly squeezed juice of 1 unwaxed lime

1–2 egg yolks (optional)

100 g/3½ oz. Parmesan cheese, finely grated

freshly ground black pepper

a plain cookie cutter, 5 cm/2 inch diameter

4 or 5 x 12-hole mini muffin tins

makes 40–50

caesar salad tarts

For those who like the garlicky crouton bit of Caesar salad best. Here the crouton is the star, with the salad cradled within. Use Little Gem or Boston lettuces, as they hold their bite and freshness well, even when chopped.

Preheat the oven to 200°C (400°F) Gas 6.

Use the cookie cutter to cut 3 or 4 rounds out of each slice of bread. Brush each round with the garlic oil and press into mini muffin tins. Bake for about 6 minutes until golden brown and toasted.

Put any remaining garlic oil in a large bowl with all the other ingredients, except the Parmesan, and toss together.

Finally, sprinkle the Parmesan into the salad to coat everything finely and pile into the crouton cases.

375 g/13 oz. ready-made
shortcrust pastry

flavoured aspic

1 sheet of leaf gelatine

150 ml/⅔ cup light fish
stock

1–2 tablespoons lemon-
flavoured vodka

2 tablespoons chopped
fresh chives

smoked salmon filling

60 ml/¼ cup sour cream

90 g/3¼ oz. smoked
salmon, chopped (or
avruga or keta caviar)

whole chives, to garnish

a plain cookie cutter,
6 cm/2½ inch diameter

2 x 12-hole mini muffin
tins

foil or baking parchment
and baking beans

makes 24

smoked salmon, vodka and sour cream tartlets

Make these pretty little tartlets for a special occasion – they simply explode with fabulous flavours. This recipe uses smoked salmon, but you can also use avruga (herring roe prepared like caviar) if you can find it – its almost smoky taste is just perfect with the hidden sour cream and chives.

Preheat the oven to 200°C (400°F) Gas 6.

Roll out the pastry as thinly as possible on a lightly floured work surface, then stamp out 24 circles with the cookie cutter. Use these to line the holes of the mini muffin tins. Prick the bases and chill or freeze for 15 minutes. Bake blind the cases following the method used on page 49.

To make the flavoured aspic, soak the leaf gelatine in cold water for 2–3 minutes until soft. Warm the fish stock, then stir in the drained gelatine until dissolved. Add the vodka. Let cool until syrupy but still pourable, then stir in the chives.

Arrange the pastry cases on a tray and add ½ teaspoon sour cream to each tartlet. Cover with a mound of smoked salmon (or a little avruga or keta caviar), then spoon in enough aspic to fill to the top of the pastry. Put in the refrigerator for 15–20 minutes to set, then garnish each one with a couple of chive stems. Serve immediately.

375 g/13 oz. ready-made shortcrust pastry

onion and garlic filling

75 g/6 tablespoons butter

600 g/1 lb 5 oz. sweet onions, sliced

1 teaspoon salt

300 ml/1¼ cups double/heavy cream or crème fraîche

2 sprigs of rosemary

6 large garlic cloves

olive oil

4 medium egg yolks

freshly grated nutmeg, to taste

2 tablespoons chopped fresh rosemary

sea salt and freshly ground black pepper

30 Greek-style black olives, chopped, or rosemary sprigs, to serve

6 individual tartlet tins or 15 mini ones (you could use a mini muffin tin)

foil or baking parchment and baking beans

makes 6 tartlets or 12–15 mini tartlets

onion, rosemary and roasted garlic tartlets

Toasting the whole garlic cloves in oil gives them a sweet nuttiness, and almost caramelizes them. They are blended with lots of rosemary, then cooked in the mini tartlet shells to make deliciously rustic appetizers.

Preheat the oven to 200°C (400°F) Gas 6.

Roll out the pastry thinly on a lightly floured surface and use to line the tart tins, then prick the bases, chill or freeze for 15 minutes, and bake blind following the method used on page 49.

Melt the butter in a large saucepan and add the onions, stirring to coat. Add a few tablespoons of water and the 1 teaspoon salt, and cover with a lid. Steam very gently for 30 minutes to 1 hour (trying not to look too often!) until meltingly soft. When the onions are cooked, remove the lid and cook for a few minutes to evaporate any excess liquid – the mixture should be quite thick. Let cool.

Put the cream or crème fraîche and rosemary leaves into a saucepan and heat until almost boiling. Remove from the heat and leave to infuse for as long as possible.

Put the garlic cloves into a small saucepan and just cover with olive oil. Simmer over gentle heat for 40 minutes or until the garlic is golden and soft.

Remove the garlic from the oil (which you can keep to make salad dressings). Strain the cooled flavoured cream into a blender and add the cooked garlic and egg yolks. Season to taste with salt, pepper and nutmeg, and blend until smooth. Stir in the chopped rosemary.

Set the tartlet cases on a baking sheet. Spoon the cooled onions evenly into the cases, filling just half full. Pour the rosemary and garlic cream over the top. Bake for 15–20 minutes (depending on size) or until set and pale golden brown. Serve warm, topped with chopped black olives or a sprig of rosemary.

½ French baguette

olive oil, for brushing

100 g/3½ oz. Gorgonzola cheese

1 pear, peeled, halved, cored and cut into 12 thin wedges

12 walnut halves (optional)

makes 12

blue cheese and pear crostini

Creamy, piquant Gorgonzola and sweet, juicy pear are a perfect pairing on these crisp, bite-sized crostini. These are ideal for serving at a sophisticated tea party, or as Christmassy canapés.

Cut 12 thin slices from the baguette – they should be no more than 1 cm/½ inch thick. Brush each one with a little oil then toast under a preheated grill/broiler until crisp and golden on both sides. Let cool.

When ready to serve, top each crostini with a pear wedge, a thin slice of Gorgonzola and a walnut half (if using).

pinchos

2 tablespoons olive oil

1 garlic clove, crushed

½ teaspoon chilli/hot red pepper flakes

leaves from 2 sprigs of thyme

100 g/3½ oz. white asparagus, in can or jar

2 tablespoons ground almonds

½ canned pimiento, chopped

8 slices of white bread, lightly toasted

sea salt and freshly ground black pepper

serves 4

Pinchos originate from Spain and are a tapas classic, often served in bars. These tasty little morsels are also ideal party bites and are really simple to make.

Put the oil, garlic, chilli/hot red pepper flakes and thyme in a saucepan, heat through to flavour the oil, then remove from the heat and let cool.

Put the asparagus in a blender and pulse until smooth. Slowly add the strained oil and blend again. Mix in the ground almonds and salt and pepper to taste.

Slice the pimiento into thin strips. Spoon the asparagus mixture onto the sliced bread and top with the sliced pimiento. Add a few thyme leaves and serve on a tray for your guests to help themselves.

goats' cheese and pepper crostini

1 thin French breadstick (ficelle)

150 g/5½ oz. fresh creamy goats' cheese

4 roasted red bell peppers, peeled

40 spears Thai asparagus, cooked and refreshed in cold water

olive oil, for brushing

sea salt and freshly ground black pepper

makes 20

These pretty bites are a breeze to prepare. You can bake the ficelle and assemble the crostini up to 1 hour in advance and simply cover and chill until required.

Preheat the oven to 190°C (375°F) Gas 5.

To make the crostini, slice the breadstick diagonally into 20 thin slices. Brush the slices with olive oil, then sprinkle with salt and pepper. Cook in the preheated oven for 5 minutes until golden.

Arrange the crostini on a plate and spread with goats' cheese. Cut the roasted peppers into thin strips, then arrange a strip of pepper and 2 spears of asparagus on each crostini. Serve.

pea and parma ham crostini

The new season's peas are so deliciously sweet. Use them to prepare this brilliantly colourful spread which makes a perfect topping for crostini.

crostini

1 ready-to-bake ciabatta loaf

olive oil spray or 2–3 tablespoons light olive oil

topping

250 g/2 cups shelled fresh or frozen peas

2 spring onions/scallions

40 g/1½ oz. aged pecorino or Parmesan cheese, finely grated

1 tablespoon finely chopped fresh mint or dill

2 tablespoons fruity olive oil

freshly squeezed lemon juice

125 g/4½ oz. finely sliced Parma ham, prosciutto or other air dried ham, torn or cut into half

sea salt and freshly ground black pepper

makes 16–18

Preheat the oven to 180°C (350°F) Gas 4. Cut the ciabatta on the slant into fairly thin slices. Spray both sides with olive oil or pour the olive oil onto a baking sheet and dip the slices of ciabatta in it. Bake for 15 minutes, turning the slices halfway through.

Cook the peas in boiling water for 2–3 minutes or until just tender and then drain them under cold running water. Trim and cut the spring onions/scallions in half lengthways then slice very finely. Put the peas and spring onions/scallions in a food processor and pulse until you get a chunky spread. Add the pecorino, mint or dill and pulse again then stir in the olive oil. Season to taste with salt, pepper and a good squeeze of lemon.

Spread the mixture thickly on the ciabatta toasts, drape with a piece of ham and serve.

baby rarebits with beetroot and orange relish

These baby rarebits are real old-fashioned comfort food for an old-fashioned afternoon tea. Topped with jewel-coloured beetroot relish, they make a pretty addition to the tea table. Choose a well-flavoured cheese to fully appreciate the contrast of sweet, sharp and tangy tastes.

To make the beetroot and orange relish, heat the olive oil in a frying pan/skillet and gently fry the shallot for about 3 minutes. Add the ginger and cardamom seeds and fry for another minute. Add the beetroot, apple and orange juice, and season well with salt and pepper. Cook very gently, stirring frequently, for about 20 minutes until tender and moist, but not wet. Check and adjust the seasoning, if necessary, then set aside.

Cut 12 thin slices of baguette on the diagonal, about 1 cm/½ inch thick. Put the wine, cheese and mustard in a small saucepan and heat gently, until the cheese has melted. Season with black pepper, beat in the egg yolks and set aside.

Grill/broil the slices of baguette on one side until golden. Turn over, spoon on the cheese mixture and grill/broil for another 2–3 minutes until golden and bubbling. Transfer to a serving plate, top with the relish, sprinkle with dill sprigs and serve immediately.

1 small baguette

3 tablespoons white wine

100 g/3½ oz. mature Cheddar cheese, grated

1 teaspoon Dijon mustard

2 egg yolks

freshly ground black pepper

fresh dill sprigs, to garnish

beetroot and orange relish

1 tablespoon olive oil

1 shallot, finely chopped

1 teaspoon grated fresh ginger

seeds of 2 cardamom pods, crushed

1 beetroot, peeled and grated

¼ cooking apple, peeled, cored and grated

freshly squeezed juice of 1 orange

salt and freshly ground black pepper

makes 12

lemon buffalo mozzarella and pickled figs on crostini

When you can get them, ripe figs are a delicious alternative to dried. Only use the best, freshest buffalo mozzarella for this recipe. This topping also works well on toasted ciabatta.

1–2 baguettes, each cut into 1-cm/½-inch slices

pickled figs

400 ml/1⅔ cups rosé wine

100 ml/6 tablespoons sweet raspberry vinegar

1 small fresh red chilli

1 clove

6 dried lavender heads

250 g/9 oz. soft dried figs (about 10), quartered

lemon buffalo mozzarella

2–3 tablespoons extra virgin olive oil

grated zest and freshly squeezed juice of 1 small unwaxed lemon

1 teaspoon sea salt crystals

250 g/9 oz. buffalo mozzarella (about 2 balls)

2 baking sheets

makes about 20

To make the pickled figs, put all the ingredients except the figs in a saucepan and reduce the liquid by half over medium heat. Remove from the heat, add the figs and let cool.

For the mozzarella, pour the olive oil into a bowl and mix with the lemon zest and juice and the salt crystals. Tear the mozzarella in half and in half again, repeating until you have enough pieces to match your fig halves. If the mozzarella is very soft, tear it in half then cut it with scissors. Gently coat the mozzarella in the lemon mixture and leave for 1 hour to infuse.

Preheat the oven to 200°C (400°F) Gas 6.

To make the crostini, bake the bread slices on baking sheets in the preheated oven for about 10–15 minutes until golden.

To assemble, put a piece of infused mozzarella and a pickled fig quarter on each crostini so they lean against each other. Serve immediately.

smoked oyster and goats' cheese pastries

250 g/9 oz. ready-made puff pastry

100 g/3½ oz. soft, rindless goat's' cheese, crumbled

170 g/6 oz. canned smoked oysters

1 egg, beaten

sea salt and freshly ground black pepper

a baking sheet, greased

serves 12

Smoked oysters are a relatively inexpensive way to enjoy a traditionally extravagant delicacy, and are much under-used. These delicious little pastries can be made up to 4 hours in advance of a party.

Roll out the pastry on a lightly floured surface until very thin, to make a rectangle, then cut the pastry in half lengthways.

Put half the crumbled goats' cheese down the middle of one piece of pastry. Arrange half the oysters in a row on top of the goats' cheese. Brush the beaten egg along both the long sides, fold the pastry over lengthways and gently press the edges together to seal. Repeat with the other piece of pastry and remaining cheese and oysters.

Lightly brush both pastry parcels with beaten egg, then sprinkle with salt and pepper. Cut both parcels into 3-cm/1-inch thick slices, then transfer to the greased baking sheet. Cook in a preheated oven at 200°C (400°F) Gas 6 for 12 minutes until puffed and golden. Let cool to room temperature before serving.

about 250 g/9 oz. ready-rolled shortcrust pastry

4 baby artichoke hearts in olive oil, drained and cut into quarters

50 g/2 oz. buffalo mozzarella, drained and cut into 16 pieces

8 cherry tomatoes, halved

2 spring onions/scallions, each cut into 8 pieces

1 egg yolk, lightly beaten

sea salt and freshly ground black pepper

2 baking sheets, greased

makes 16

artichoke and tomato pastry boats

Using ready-rolled pastry for this recipe makes it the height of simplicity. However, preparing the delicate squares of pastry can be time-consuming so enlist some help to put these together. They can be made up to 2 hours in advance.

Preheat the oven to 180°C (350°F) Gas 4.

Put the ready-rolled pastry on a lightly floured work surface. Using a sharp knife, cut the pastry into 16 pieces, each measuring about 3.5 cm/1½ inches square. Transfer to the baking sheets.

Put a piece of artichoke, a piece of mozzarella, a tomato half and a piece of spring onion/scallion on top of each pastry square, pushing them in lightly to secure them. Brush the edges of the pastry with egg yolk, then gently squeeze the edges together to form a boat shape. Season with salt and pepper.

Bake in the preheated oven for 12–15 minutes until golden and cooked. Serve warm or at room temperature.

350 g/12 oz. cooked, peeled prawns/shrimp

2–3 spring onions/scallions, trimmed and finely chopped

1 teaspoon finely grated fresh ginger or ginger paste

1 teaspoon finely grated fresh garlic or garlic paste

1½ teaspoons nam pla (Thai fish sauce)

2 teaspoons light soy sauce

½ teaspoon sesame oil

1 medium egg white

1 tablespoon ground rice

a pinch of sugar

about 5 thin slices white bread, preferably 2–3 days old

60–75 g/½ cup sesame seeds

sea salt and freshly ground black pepper

2 non-stick baking sheets

makes about 20

sesame prawn toasts

These simple sesame prawn toasts are much easier to handle than the classic Chinese deep fried ones and can be prepared ahead and baked at the last minute.

Put the prawns/shrimp in a food processor along with all the other ingredients except the bread and sesame seeds and whizz until smooth. Transfer to a bowl, cover and refrigerate for an hour or two for the flavours to mellow.

Preheat the oven to 230°C (450°F) Gas 8. Cut the crusts off the bread and toast lightly. Let cool then spread each slice thickly with the prawn/shrimp paste. Cut each slice of toast diagonally to make 4 triangles. Put the sesame seeds into a shallow bowl. Press the prawn/shrimp toasts upper side down lightly into the sesame seeds then lay them on baking sheets. Bake for about 5–6 minutes until the toasts are warm and the sesame seeds lightly browned. Cool for 10 minutes then serve.

fillet steak on toast with mustard and rocket

1 ciabatta loaf

2 tablespoons wholegrain mustard

2 tablespoons homemade mayonnaise or good-quality prepared mayonnaise

400 g/14 oz. beef fillet/tenderloin

1 tablespoon olive oil

50 g/2 oz. rocket/arugula

sea salt and cracked black pepper, to serve

a griddle pan/ridged stove-top grill pan

makes about 20

A satisfying combination of rare, juicy beef with mustard and peppery rocket/arugula. If you prefer, Dijon, English or honey mustard can be substituted for wholegrain.

Preheat the oven to 200°C (400°F) Gas 6.

Cut the ciabatta loaf in half lengthways and toast in the oven for about 10 minutes. Mix the mustard and mayonnaise together and spread evenly onto the cut halves of toasted ciabatta.

Brush the beef with the olive oil and heat a griddle pan/ridged stove-top grill pan. Sear the beef in the hot pan without disturbing, for about 2 minutes, and repeat on the other side. Transfer the beef to a chopping board and rest for 15 minutes.

Using a sharp knife, slice the beef into enough thin slices to cover the ciabatta. Press the beef gently onto the ciabatta, to encourage it to stick to the mustard mixture. Scatter the rocket/arugula over the beef and carefully cut into fingers. Serve with little dishes of sea salt and cracked black pepper.

flash-seared tuna on rye with horseradish and tarragon cream

2 tablespoons olive oil

1 teaspoon soft brown sugar

500 g/1 lb 2 oz. piece of fresh tuna loin, thin end

200 ml/¾ cup crème fraîche or sour cream

2 tablespoons horseradish sauce

1 carrot, grated

2 tablespoons chopped fresh tarragon, plus 20 whole leaves to serve

300 g/10½ oz. rye bread, cut into 20 fingers

sea salt and freshly ground black pepper

a griddle pan/ridged stove-top grill pan

makes 20

The richness of fresh tuna is complemented here by the sharpness of the horseradish and the aniseed pungency of tarragon. With the rye bread base, this is a substantial canapé, packed with flavour.

In a wide, shallow bowl, mix the olive oil, sugar and a little salt and pepper together, then add the tuna and turn carefully until coated.

Heat a heavy-based griddle pan/ridged stove-top grill pan over high heat until very hot. Add the tuna and, using tongs to turn it over, sear on all sides for about 1 minute. Remove from the heat and let it cool slightly before cutting into 20 thin even slices.

Mix the crème fraîche or sour cream, horseradish, carrot and chopped tarragon together in a separate bowl. Season with salt and black pepper and spread on the rye bread fingers. Top each with a slice of seared tuna and a tarragon leaf and serve immediately.

Note: if you prefer to eat tuna medium to well done, simply return the slices to the pan and sear for a further 30 seconds to 1 minute, until cooked as desired.

mini pissaladières

topping

2 tablespoons olive oil

2 large sweet onions (about 500 g/1 lb 2 oz. in total), peeled and thinly sliced

1 clove of garlic, peeled and finely chopped

1 teaspoon finely chopped fresh thyme or ½ teaspoon dried thyme

150 g/5½ oz. small, pitted marinated black olives

sea salt and freshly ground black pepper

a few small basil leaves, to decorate

pastry

100 g/3½ oz. Quark or cream cheese

100 g/7 tablespoons butter at room temperature, cubed

125 g/1 cup plain/all-purpose flour

1 level teaspoon baking powder

a good pinch of sea salt

a plain cookie cutter, 8 cm/3½ inch diameter

2 x 12-hole tartlet tins

makes about 12–14

These are great for parties as they can be baked in advance and frozen. To serve, make sure they are thawed before reheating in a moderate oven.

Heat the oil in a large casserole or saucepan. Tip in the onions then cook over a moderate heat until they have begun to collapse (about 10 minutes). Stir in the garlic and thyme, turn the heat down a little and continue to cook for another 30–40 minutes until the onions are soft and golden and any liquid has evaporated, taking care they don't catch and burn. Season with salt and pepper and set aside to cool.

While the onions are cooking make the pastry. Tip the Quark or cream cheese in a food processor with the cubed butter and process until smooth. Sift the flour with the baking powder and salt and add to the creamed cheese and butter in two batches, using the pulse to incorporate it. Once the mixture starts to form a ball, turn it out of the processor onto a floured board and form it into a flat disc. Put it in a plastic bag and chill for an hour in the refrigerator.

When ready to cook the tartlets, preheat the oven to 220°C (425°F) Gas 7. Roll out the pastry quite thinly. Using the pastry cutter, stamp rounds out of the pastry and lay them in the hollows of your tartlet tins. Spoon in teaspoons of the cooled onion mixture and top with an olive. Bake for 15–20 minutes until the pastry is puffed up and golden. Cool for 10 minutes then remove the tarts carefully from the tin and arrange on a plate. Scatter a few small basil leaves and serve.

3 tablespoons olive oil

450 g/1 lb minced/ground pork

1 onion, finely chopped

1 large clove of garlic, finely chopped

2 tablespoons tomato purée/concentrate

½ rounded teaspoon mixed spice

125 ml/½ cup passata or creamed tomatoes

1 tablespoon cider vinegar

10 large pitted green olives (about 50 g/2 oz.) marinated in garlic and herbs, finely chopped

2 tablespoons finely chopped parsley

500 g/1 lb 2 oz. bought or homemade puff pastry

plain/all-purpose flour for rolling out the pastry

1 large egg, beaten

sea salt and freshly ground black pepper

2 large baking sheets, greased

a plain cookie cutter, 8 cm/3½ inch diameter

serves 8

pork and olive empanadas

Empanadas are like mini-pasties – in fact they're believed to have been introduced to Mexico by the Cornish tin miners who came to work in the tin and silver mines.

Heat 1 tablespoon olive oil in a large frying pan/skillet and brown the pork. Remove to a bowl with a slotted spoon and pour off any remaining fat and meat juices. Add the remaining 2 tablespoons oil to the pan and fry the chopped onion for about 6–7 minutes until beginning to brown. Add the chopped garlic, fry for a few seconds then return the meat to the pan. Add the tomato purée/concentrate, stir in thoroughly and cook for a minute then add the mixed spice, passata/creamed tomatoes and cider vinegar. Bring to the boil and simmer for 10–15 minutes until the excess liquid has been absorbed.

Stir in the finely chopped olives and parsley and season to taste with salt and freshly ground pepper. Set aside until cool (about 1 hour) Unroll the pastry and roll it out thinly on a floured board or work surface. Cut out rounds with a cookie cutter, place a teaspoonful of the pork filling into the middle, dampen the edges with water, fold over and press the edges together. Repeat until you have used up all the pastry and filling, re-rolling the pastry as necessary. At this point you can refrigerate or freeze the empanadas.

To cook, preheat the oven to 220°C (425°F) Gas 7. Cut a small slit in each empanada with a sharp knife. Brush with beaten egg and place on greased baking sheets. Bake for 8–10 minutes until puffed up and golden (slightly longer if cooking them from frozen). Serve warm.

chic canapés

piquant rare duck in chicory boats with crushed peanuts

400 g/14 oz. boneless duck breast, skin on

2 tablespoons redcurrant jelly

1 teaspoon finely chopped fresh red chilli

2 teaspoons hot smoked paprika (*pimentón*)

2 garlic cloves, crushed

2 teaspoons sweet raspberry vinegar

3–4 medium chicory heads/Belgian endives

a handful of fresh basil leaves

100 g/3½ oz. dry-roasted peanuts, roughly crushed in a food processor

makes about 30

Look for small to medium chicory/endive heads to make good-sized 'boats' for this recipe. As an alternative finishing touch, try scattering over a mix of crushed salted peanuts and freshly grated coconut.

Preheat the oven to 200°C (400°F) Gas 6.

Score the duck fat (not the flesh) with a sharp knife. Cook in a hot flameproof, ovenproof pan over medium/high heat until the skin is golden brown and most of the fat has been rendered. Transfer to the oven for 10 minutes, then remove and leave to rest.

Meanwhile, mix the redcurrant jelly, chilli, paprika, garlic and vinegar together in a bowl. Remove and discard any remaining cold fat from the duck breasts, then cut them into equal slices. Put the duck slices in the bowl containing the chilli mixture and toss to coat the duck.

Cut the thick ends off the chicory/endive and separate the leaves. Line each one with a basil leaf, put a rare slice of duck on top and scatter the peanuts over. Serve with the pointed end of the leaf facing outwards on the plate.

polenta cups

175 g/1 stick plus
4 tablespoons butter

175 g/6 oz. cream cheese

280 g/2 cups plus
2 tablespoons plain/all-purpose flour

175 g/1 cup plus
2 tablespoons polenta

a pinch of sea salt crystals

black bean chilli

500 g/1 lb 2 oz. dried black beans, soaked in water overnight

2 teaspoons cumin seeds

2 teaspoons coriander seeds

2–3 tablespoons olive oil

4 shallots, finely chopped

3 garlic cloves, crushed

1 fresh green chilli, chopped

1 fresh red chilli, chopped

1 teaspoon soft brown sugar

2 teaspoons sea salt

50 g/2 oz. dark chocolate, grated

1 tablespoon tomato purée/concentrate

1 tablespoon chopped fresh coriander/cilantro

400 ml/1⅔ cup crème fraîche or sour cream

smoked paprika, to sprinkle

4 or 5 x 12-hole mini muffin tins

makes about 60

black bean chilli in polenta cups with crème fraîche

This canapé is so useful because the cups and chilli can be made in advance. The polenta cups can be frozen, while the chilli can be made on the day, refrigerated, and then warmed through when you are ready to assemble and serve it.

Preheat the oven to 180°C (350°F) Gas 4.

First make the polenta cups. Cream the butter and cream cheese together. Combine the flour, polenta and salt and add to the butter and cream cheese gradually, until the mixture forms a dough. Break off 3-cm/1½-inch balls and neatly press into the mini muffin tins, forming a cup shape. Bake for 20 minutes until golden.

To make the chilli, put the drained black beans in a large saucepan of fresh cold water, bring to the boil and cook for 1–1½ hours until tender. In a large heavy-based saucepan warm the spice seeds until just starting to pop, then remove from the pan and set aside. Gently heat the olive oil in the same pan and add the shallots, garlic and chillies. After 5 minutes add the sugar, salt, chocolate and tomato purée/concentrate and cook for a further 2–3 minutes.

Remove from the heat and allow to cool slightly, then blend in a food processor with the warmed spice seeds. Combine this mixture, the drained black beans and fresh coriander/cilantro in a large bowl. Spoon into the polenta cups, top with crème fraîche or sour cream and sprinkle over a little paprika, to serve.

butternut squash hot shots

3 tablespoons olive oil

1 onion, chopped

5 garlic cloves, crushed

1 fresh red chilli, deseeded and chopped

1 teaspoon ras-el-hanout or mild curry powder

1 kg/2 lb 4 oz. butternut squash, peeled, deseeded and chopped into chunks

1 litre/4 cups vegetable stock

100 g/3½ oz. sun-blush/half-dried tomatoes in olive oil, drained

300 ml/1¼ cups fresh apple juice

300 ml/1¼ cups sour cream

sea salt and freshly ground black pepper

shot glasses

makes 40–50 shots

Offer friends a warm welcome on cold, dark nights with these little soup shots, warm in colour, taste and temperature. Make sure your shot glasses are thick enough to contain hot liquids safely.

Heat the olive oil in a large, heavy-based saucepan and gently fry the onion, garlic, chilli and ras-el-hanout for a couple of minutes. Add the squash and fry for a further 5 minutes. Pour in the stock and cook for 10–12 minutes until the squash is tender. Remove from the heat and set aside to cool. Transfer the cooled squash to a food processor and add the tomatoes, apple juice and half the sour cream. Blend until very smooth. Season to taste.

When you are ready to serve, reheat the soup and use the remaining sour cream to bring it to drinking consistency. Try one before serving; if the soup is too thick it will stay in the glass so add a little more cream or water to thin it further. You can also embellish the soup. Here are a few easy spiking suggestions:

• A crispy piece of pan-fried pancetta laid over the rim

• A couple of drops of white truffle oil on top

• A dash of Madeira or Marsala added just before serving

• A little coriander/cilantro oil and a few chopped leaves stirred in

• A few drops of sweet chilli sauce added

• A thin wedge of Stilton balanced across the glass

courgette rolls

2 courgettes/zucchini

2 tablespoons olive oil

1 teaspoon freshly squeezed lemon juice

75 g/2½ oz. creamy Gorgonzola cheese

75 g/2½ oz. ricotta cheese

30 g/¼ cup walnuts, finely chopped

12 fresh mint leaves

small handful of fresh chives, cut into 5-cm/2-inch lengths

chilli oil, for sprinkling

freshly ground black pepper

a griddle/ridged stove-top grill pan

makes 12

Griddled courgette/zucchini slices make an ideal wrap for a stylish appetizer which is packed full of flavour. You can also try Roquefort or dolcelatte cheese as alternatives to the Gorgonzola.

Trim the ends off the courgettes/zucchini and cut a thin slice, lengthways, off each side and discard. Then cut each vegetable into six slices lengthways, about 5 mm/¼ inch thick. Mix the olive oil and lemon juice together. Brush over the courgette/zucchini slices and sprinkle with freshly ground black pepper.

Heat a griddle/ridged stove-top grill pan for about 4 minutes, or until hot. Put half the courgette/zucchini slices in the pan and cook until the underneath has developed brown lines from the ridges in the pan. Turn over and repeat on the other side, but do not overcook or they may split when rolled. Transfer to a plate to cool and cook the remaining courgette/zucchini slices.

Mix the Gorgonzola and ricotta cheeses together and spread over the courgette/zucchini slices. Sprinkle each with a few chopped walnuts and place a mint leaf and a few chives at one end, so they overlap the edge. Starting from this end, gently roll up.

Arrange the rolls on serving plates with the mint and chives uppermost. Serve the rolls sprinkled with a little chilli oil and freshly ground black pepper.

20–25 baby plum tomatoes

1 tablespoon caster/superfine sugar

400 g/14 oz. ready-rolled puff pastry, thawed if frozen

4 tablespoons olive oil

150-g/5½-oz. goats' cheese log with rind (not too ripe)

freshly ground black pepper

small fresh basil leaves, to serve

black olive tapenade

100 g/⅔ cup pitted black olives

20 g/2 tablespoons capers

1 tablespoon anchovy paste

1 garlic clove, crushed

1 tablespoon olive oil

1 teaspoon sea salt

1 teaspoon chopped fresh thyme

2 baking sheets, greased

a plain cookie cutter, 4 cm/1½ inch diameter

makes 40–50

slow-roasted tomato galettes with black olive tapenade and goats' cheese

These sweet-tasting tomatoes are delicious so you could always make more than you need and keep them in the refrigerator to enjoy on another day. Replace the tomatoes and tapenade with slow-roasted black grapes and onion confit as an alternative idea.

Preheat the oven to 140°C (275°F) Gas 1.

Cut the baby plum tomatoes in half lengthways, season with the sugar and black pepper and put on an oiled baking sheet. Bake in the preheated oven for 2 hours. Remove the tomatoes from the oven and leave to cool.

Turn the oven temperature up to 200°C (400°F) Gas 6. Brush the puff pastry with the olive oil, prick all over with a fork and stamp out 40–50 discs using the cookie cutter and put them on baking sheets. Cook for 10–15 minutes, turning over halfway through. Remove from the oven but leave the heat on.

Put all the tapenade ingredients in a food processor and blend to mix. Cover and set aside until needed.

Thinly slice the goats' cheese into 40–50 rounds or pieces depending on the diameter of the log (to make this easier, chill the cheese beforehand).

To assemble the galettes, spread a little tapenade onto each cooked pastry disc. Top with a goats' cheese slice and tomato half. Return to the oven for about 5 minutes to warm through, then serve topped with a basil leaf.

sticky dates with lemon feta and walnuts

These canapés are refreshing, zesty and perfect served with cocktails. Put the finished dates in the freezer for 5 minutes before serving; it somehow intensifies their honeyed sweetness. For meat lovers or those with nut allergies, chorizo is a great substitute for the walnuts.

Cut the feta into 40 little blocks or mash it, as preferred. Put in a bowl with the lemon zest and juice and add salt to taste. Let stand for 30 minutes, turning occasionally.

Put a block or a small amount of mashed feta at one end of each date half, then add a walnut half to overlap the cheese. Grind a little black pepper over the top and finish with a mint leaf.

200 g/7 oz. Greek feta cheese

grated zest of 1 unwaxed lemon and freshly squeezed juice of ½

20 Medjool dates, halved and stoned

100 g/3½ oz. walnut halves or diced chorizo sausage

sea salt and freshly ground black pepper

fresh mint leaves, to serve

makes 40

vermouth scallops with green olive tapenade

500 g/1lb 2 oz. fresh scallops (about 30–40)

3 tablespoons dry vermouth

2 tablespoons olive oil

90 g/⅔ cup green olives, stoned

3 spring onions/scallions, chopped

1 garlic clove

1 tablespoon chopped fresh parsley

1 cured chorizo sausage (about 300 g/10½ oz.)

sea salt and freshly ground black pepper

a griddle pan/ridged stove-top grill pan

cocktail sticks/toothpicks

makes 30–40

Confirmed martini lovers will enjoy this one; it's a fitting canapé to kick off a party. These can also be served on sticks or on slices of cucumber; one large cucumber is sufficient for this quantity of scallops.

Put the scallops in a large bowl with 1 tablespoon of the vermouth, the olive oil and a pinch of salt and pepper and let sit for 10 minutes.

Heat a griddle pan/ridged stove-top grill pan over high heat until very hot and sear the scallops for a minute on each side. Do not move the scallops during cooking, or they will tear.

Put all the remaining ingredients, except the chorizo, in a food processor with ½ teaspoon salt and give it a few short sharp blasts until the tapenade mixture looks chopped but not too mushy. Slice the chorizo so you have a slice for each scallop (not too thinly as you want it to support the weight of the scallops).

To assemble the canapés, spoon a little tapenade onto each chorizo slice, put a seared scallop on top and secure with a cocktail stick/toothpick to serve.

9 small sheets filo/phyllo pastry

50 g/4 tablespoons butter, melted

spicy crab filling

200 g/7 oz. canned white crab meat in brine, drained

75 g/3 oz. canned water chestnuts, drained and finely chopped or sliced

2.5-cm/1-inch piece fresh ginger, peeled and cut into fine strips

2 spring onions/scallions, trimmed and finely sliced

finely grated zest and juice of 1 unwaxed lime

1 garlic clove, crushed

½ fresh red chilli, deseeded and finely chopped

2 teaspoons sesame oil

2 tablespoons chopped fresh coriander/cilantro

sea salt and freshly ground black pepper

3 x 12-hole mini muffin tins, brushed with melted butter

makes about 36

spicy crab cups

These delicate bites are as light as air, but packed with fresh Asian flavours. Canned white crab meat from the Pacific is ideal for these – not only does it taste very good, but there is no shell or messy bits to deal with if catering for a large number of people. It is also much cheaper than fresh crab.

Preheat the oven to 180°C (350°F) Gas 4.

Unroll the filo/phyllo pastry and cut the stack into 108 squares, each measuring 7 x 7 cm/3 x 3 inches. To do this, keep the sheets stacked on top of each other, then mark the top sheet into 12 squares. Cut down through all the layers, giving 108 squares. Pile into 2–3 stacks and keep beside you in a plastic bag.

To make a filo/phyllo cup, take 3 squares of pastry, brush each with melted butter and lay one on top of the other, so that the points make a star, and do not touch each other. Quickly but gently press into one of the holes of the prepared muffin tin, so the points of the filo/phyllo shoot upwards like a handkerchief. Repeat with all the remaining pastry until you have 36 cups.

Bake in the oven for about 8–10 minutes until golden. Remove, let cool in the tin, then carefully remove to a tray (they are very fragile).

Put the crab into a bowl and fluff up with a fork. Stir in the water chestnuts, ginger and spring onions/scallions. In a separate bowl, mix the lime zest and juice, crushed garlic, chilli and sesame oil, and season to taste. Mix this into the crab mixture (this can be done up to 4 hours in advance), then stir in the coriander/cilantro.

Fill the cups with the crab mixture just before serving (they can go a little soggy if they are kept too long).

prawn cocktail shots

200 g/¾ cup crème fraîche or sour cream

2 tablespoons tomato ketchup

2 teaspoons Manzanilla sherry

a small handful each of fresh tarragon leaves and fresh dill, chopped

1 teaspoon smoked paprika (*pimentón*)

a pinch of celery salt

2 spring onions/scallions, chopped (optional)

400 g/14 oz. cooked and peeled king prawns/jumbo shrimp (about 60), tails left on if liked

1 tablespoon snipped fresh chives or a pinch of smoked paprika (*pimentón*), to garnish

shot glasses

cocktail sticks/toothpicks

makes 30

These miniature prawn cocktails are eye-catching and popular, and an up-to-date version of a Seventies classic. You will need small shot glasses and good-looking cocktail sticks.

To make the cocktail sauce, put the crème fraîche or sour cream, ketchup, sherry, herbs, paprika and celery salt in a small bowl. Mix with a fork or small whisk until well combined and smooth.

Spoon a little cocktail sauce into each shot glass and add a few chopped spring onions/scallions, if using. Thread 2 prawns/shrimp onto each cocktail stick/toothpick. Dip the prawns/shrimp into the remaining cocktail sauce, ensuring that they are coated, then carefully slide each stick into a shot glass, being careful not to smear sauce on the inside of the glass.

Garnish with either a sprinkling of chives or a pinch of smoked paprika, as preferred. Serve immediately.

blinis with sour cream and caviar

75 g/½ cup plain/all-purpose flour

75 g/½ cup buckwheat flour

1 teaspoon baking powder

a good pinch of sea salt

1 egg

200 ml/¾ cup milk

25 g/2 tablespoons butter, melted, plus extra for greasing

for the topping

80 ml/⅓ cup sour cream or crème fraîche

½ teaspoon finely grated lemon zest

2–3 tablespoons caviar, salmon roe (or roughly chopped smoked salmon, if preferred)

freshly ground black pepper

makes about 30

Traditional Russian blinis are made with a yeasted batter, but these are leavened with baking powder and are much quicker to make. They provide the perfect base for the sour cream and salty caviar, which explodes tantalizingly on your tongue. If you are short of time, you can buy ready-made blinis to warm up in the oven.

Put the sour cream in a bowl and add the lemon zest. Stir to combine, then cover and store in the fridge until needed.

Set a frying pan/skillet over low heat. Combine the flours, baking powder and salt in a bowl and make a well in the centre. Beat together the egg, milk and melted butter, then pour into the well. Gradually work in the flour, using a fork to make a smooth batter.

Lightly grease the frying pan/skillet with butter, using a piece of kitchen paper. Drop small spoonfuls of the blini batter into the pan. Cook for about 2 minutes, until bubbles appear on the surface, then flip over and cook for a further minute, or until golden. As you make the blinis, keep them warm in a low oven.

To serve, top each blini with a little sour cream and about ¼ teaspoon of caviar. Grind a little black pepper on top and serve immediately.

scotch pancakes with smoked salmon

125 g/1 cup plain/all-purpose flour

1 teaspoon baking powder

a large pinch of salt

1 egg

150–200 ml/⅔–¾ cup milk

1–2 tablespoons sunflower/safflower oil

to serve

200 g/7 oz. smoked salmon

10 teaspoons crème fraîche or sour cream

1 tablespoon finely snipped chives

makes about 20

As well as making great canapés, you could easily serve a few of these as a fancy starter on Christmas day. The pancakes can be made in advance and frozen – simply wrap them in foil and warm in the oven before serving.

Sift the flour, baking powder and salt into a large mixing bowl. Break the egg into the bowl and gradually pour in the milk, mixing all the time with a balloon whisk. You may not need to add all the milk – the batter should be smooth and thick.

Preheat a griddle pan or heavy frying pan/skillet over medium heat. Pour a little of the oil in the pan and swirl it to coat the base of the pan evenly. Leave it to heat up.

Drop a tablespoon of batter into the hot pan for each pancake – you will probably only be able to cook 4 pancakes at a time. Cook for about 1 minute, or until bubbles start to appear on the surface and the underside is golden. Using a fish slice or palette knife, flip the pancakes over and cook the other side until the pancakes are golden.

Remove the pancakes from the pan and keep them warm on a plate covered with foil while you cook the remaining batter.

To serve, snip the smoked salmon into pieces. Dollop ½ teaspoon crème fraîche or sour cream onto each pancake and top with the salmon. Finish with a sprinkle of snipped chives.

smoked salmon and cucumber sushi rolls

375 g/scant 2 cups Japanese sushi rice

2 tablespoons sugar

1 teaspoon sea salt

4 tablespoons rice wine vinegar

1 large cucumber, unwaxed if possible

5 sheets dried nori seaweed

200 g/7 oz. sliced smoked salmon

3 teaspoons wasabi paste

to serve

Japanese pickled ginger

Japanese soy sauce, such as tamari

wasabi paste

a sushi mat or a clean cloth

serves 6

Smoked salmon fillet (sometimes known as royal fillet) is best to use for this. It is very meaty and you can cut it to the size you want. The uncut rolls can be wrapped up tightly in clingfilm, then cut and unwrapped at the last moment to preserve the freshness.

Put the rice in a sieve and wash well under running water until the water runs clear. Drain well and tip into a saucepan. Add 600 ml/2½ cups water and bring to the boil. Boil fast for 5 minutes, reduce the heat, cover and cook slowly for 10 minutes until all the water has been absorbed.

Meanwhile, put the sugar, salt and vinegar in a bowl and stir until dissolved. Tip the cooked rice onto a plate or tray and sprinkle with the vinegar mixture. Mix lightly with your hands, then let cool.

Cut the cucumber into strips the length of the long side of the nori.

To make the sushi rolls, put a sheet of nori shiny side down on a sushi mat or clean cloth. Spread one-fifth of the rice over the nori, leaving a clear strip down one long edge. Cover the rice with a thin layer of smoked salmon and spread with a little wasabi paste (thin it down with a little water if you like). Put a cucumber strip along the side opposite the clear strip of seaweed. Dampen the clear end.

Starting from the cucumber end, and using the mat to help you, roll up like a Swiss/jelly roll, sealing it into a secure cylinder with the dampened edge. Using a very sharp knife, cut into 2-cm/1-inch lengths. Repeat with the remaining seaweed, rice and salmon. Serve with pickled ginger, soy sauce and more wasabi for dipping.

sticks & skewers

500 g/1 lb 2 oz. skinless, boneless chicken breast, cubed

300 g/1¼ cups coconut cream

2 garlic cloves, crushed

1 small fresh red chilli, deseeded and chopped

30 g/1 oz. fresh piece ginger, peeled and finely grated

1 star anise

seeds from 20 cardamom pods

2 teaspoons sea salt

to serve

2 tablespoons onion seeds

a handful fresh coriander/cilantro, lightly chopped

6 long skewers, soaked in water for 30 minutes before use if wooden

cocktail sticks/toothpicks

makes 30–40

coconut and cardamom chicken

The coconut cream tenderizes the chicken, making it creamy and light, while cardamom adds an aromatic edge. It takes a little time to collect the cardamom seeds; use a rolling pin to crush the pods. These are luscious eaten hot or cold, so you could make them in advance, too.

Mix everything, except the salt, together in a bowl. Let marinate in the fridge for a few hours or overnight.

When you are ready to cook the chicken, preheat the oven to 200°C (400°F) Gas 6.

Add the salt to the cubes of chicken and toss to mix, then thread the pieces onto skewers. Arrange them in a single layer on a baking sheet. If you are using wooden skewers, cover them loosely with foil to prevent them from scorching. Cook in the oven for about 10 minutes until the chicken is cooked through.

Remove the chicken pieces from the skewers, scatter with the onion seeds and coriander/cilantro and serve on cocktail sticks/toothpicks.

chicken skewers
with sweet chilli

**12 boneless, skinless
chicken breasts**

**400 ml/1⅔ cups sweet
chilli sauce**

olive oil, for brushing

24 bamboo satay sticks,
soaked in water for 30
minutes before use

serves 24

Chicken skewers are always very popular, so it's worth
making extra. You can use boneless chicken thighs, but
always remove any excess fat (they may also need to
cook for a little longer, as the meat is denser). They can
be made the day before the party, just cover them and
chill until needed. If you want to serve them hot, put
them on a baking sheet and cook at 180°C (350°F)
Gas 4 for 12 minutes before serving.

Cut each chicken breast into 10 cubes. Put the chicken cubes in
a bowl, add the sweet chilli sauce and mix well. Cover and chill
overnight. When ready to cook, thread the chicken cubes onto the
soaked satay sticks. Heat the grill/broiler to medium-high, then brush
the rack of the grill/broiler pan with oil.

Add the chicken sticks to the rack and cook, in batches if necessary,
turning frequently, for 25 minutes, or until the chicken is cooked
through. Repeat until all the chicken skewers are cooked, then serve
hot or cold.

twice-marinated salt lime chicken

Something magical happens when you put lime and salt together. Whet guests' appetites with this zingy, salty chicken canapé. Serve chilled with icy beers and wines, or the classic Mexican drink, the margarita.

500 g/1 lb 2 oz. skinless, boneless chicken thighs

3 tablespoons olive oil

a generous pinch of salt crystals

grated zest and freshly squeezed juice of 2 unwaxed limes

lime wedges, to serve

cocktail sticks/toothpicks

makes 40

Cut the chicken into 40 even chunks and put it in a non-metallic dish with 1 tablespoon of the olive oil, half the salt crystals and the zest and juice of 1 lime. Let marinate in the fridge for 2 hours.

When you are ready to cook, remove the chicken from the marinade. Heat the remaining olive oil in a frying pan/skillet and sauté the chicken over medium heat for about 5 minutes until cooked through, shaking the pan occasionally. Put in a clean dish with the remaining salt and lime zest and juice. Mix and chill for 1 hour before serving with small forks or cocktail sticks/toothpicks and wedges of lime.

peppered duck, fig and bay skewers

500 g/1 lb 2 oz. lean duck breasts

2 garlic cloves crushed with 1 teaspoon sea salt

25 soft dried figs, halved (about 500g/1 lb 2 oz.)

50 bay leaves

2 tablespoons olive oil

freshly ground black pepper

50 wooden skewers, soaked in water for 30 minutes before use

2 baking sheets

makes 50

This one is favoured by meat lovers and Francophiles. Use loin of lamb for a change or if you cannot find duck. For vegetarians, use big flat mushrooms. They look great on earthy yellow or terracotta dishes.

Preheat the oven to 200°C (400°F) Gas 6.

Cut the duck breasts into 50 strips of approximately the same size. Using clean hands, mix all the remaining ingredients together in a bowl, then add the duck strips and mix well.

Thread a duck strip and fig half on each skewer, with a bay leaf in between. Put the skewers on baking sheets, loosely covering the ends with foil to prevent them from scorching. Cook in the oven for 5–6 minutes, turning once, until the duck is tender and cooked through. Serve warm.

spicy moorish skewers

2 tablespoons olive oil

2 garlic cloves, crushed

1 dried red chilli, crushed

1 teaspoon ground cumin

1 teaspoon ground fennel

1 teaspoon smoked sweet paprika (*pimentón dulce*)

freshly squeezed juice of 1 lemon

2 tablespoons freshly chopped flat leaf parsley

1 tablespoon dry sherry

500 g/1 lb 2 oz. lean pork fillet/tenderloin

metal skewers, or bamboo, soaked in water for 30 minutes before use

serves 4

This recipe is from Andalusia, where you see it in almost every tapas bar. The area is renowned for simple food, so this is a quick, easy recipe which leaves more time for other things, like chatting with friends.

Put the oil, garlic, chilli, cumin, fennel, paprika, lemon juice, parsley and sherry in a bowl and mix well. Cut the pork into 2.5-cm/1-inch cubes and add to the bowl. Mix well so that all the meat is covered in the marinade, cover and chill overnight in the refrigerator.

When ready to cook, preheat a grill/broiler until very hot. Thread the pork onto the skewers and grill for 10 minutes, turning often – take care not to overcook the meat. Remove from the heat and set aside for 10 minutes. Serve warm.

1 litre/4 cups grapeseed oil

pork balls

500 g/1 lb 2 oz. pork mince/ground pork

1 egg

2 teaspoons ground allspice

10 fresh sage leaves, chopped

50 g/2 oz. spring onions/scallions, chopped

1 teaspoon cayenne pepper

2 teaspoons sea salt

1 teaspoon caraway seeds

2 teaspoons tomato purée/concentrate

2 tablespoons goose fat or olive oil

cider syrup

500 ml/2 cups sweet apple cider

100 ml/6 tablespoons balsamic vinegar

1 small fresh red or green chilli

cocktail sticks/toothpicks

makes 40–50

spiced pork balls with sticky cider syrup

These subtly spiced pork balls are always a winner. The goose fat or olive oil keeps them succulent while cooking. If you have an electric deep-fat fryer, you'll find these even easier to make.

To make the pork balls, put all the ingredients in a large bowl and mix together thoroughly. Using clean hands, roll into 40–50 small balls and chill in the refrigerator for an hour.

For the cider syrup, put the cider and balsamic vinegar in a heavy-based saucepan, bring to the boil, then reduce the heat and simmer until reduced by about half to a syrupy consistency. Add the chilli and leave to infuse. (Remember to remove the chilli before serving.)

When you are ready to cook the pork balls, preheat the oven to 200°C (400°F) Gas 6.

Pour the grapeseed oil into a deep, heavy-based saucepan and heat for deep-frying. To test the oil, drop in a crust of bread. If it sizzles immediately and turns golden brown it is ready; if it browns too much turn the heat down a little. Deep-fry the pork balls in 3 or 4 batches for a couple of minutes. Remove with a slotted spoon and drain on kitchen paper. Transfer to a shallow ovenproof dish and cook in the oven for a further 5–7 minutes until cooked all the way through. Serve with cocktail sticks/toothpicks and the sticky cider syrup in a small bowl for dipping.

grilled lamb skewers with garlic and saffron custard

500 g/1 lb 2 oz. lamb
loin fillet, cut into 30
cubes

2 tablespoons olive oil

1 tablespoon chopped
fresh oregano

freshly ground black
pepper

garlic and saffron
custard

50 g/3 tablespoons
butter

8–10 garlic cloves,
coarsely grated

½ teaspoon saffron
strands

500 ml/2 cups
double/heavy cream

grated zest and freshly
squeezed juice of 1 small
unwaxed lemon

sea salt, to taste

30 short wooden skewers,
soaked in water for 30
minutes before use

makes 30

The wonderful garlic and saffron dipping sauce has the consistency of custard, but doesn't actually contain eggs. If the custard becomes too thick, dilute it with a little lemon juice or white wine.

Marinate the lamb in the olive oil, oregano and black pepper for about 2 hours.

When you are ready to cook the lamb, preheat the grill/broiler to medium.

Thread the lamb cubes onto the prepared wooden skewers and put them on a baking sheet, loosely covering the sticks with foil to prevent them from scorching. Set aside.

To make the custard, gently heat the butter, garlic and saffron together in a large, heavy-based frying pan/skillet. Add half the cream and simmer until the cream bubbles and thickens, then add the lemon juice and turn down the heat.

Grill/broil the lamb skewers for 2–3 minutes on each side and keep warm until ready to serve.

Add the remaining cream, the lemon zest and salt to the saffron cream mixture and stir over low heat until you have a custard-like sauce. Pour into a bowl and serve with the aromatic lamb skewers.

tomato aioli

3 egg yolks

2 garlic cloves

75 g/2½ oz. sun-dried
or sun-blush (half-dried)
tomatoes in oil, drained

freshly squeezed juice
of 1 lemon

1 teaspoon tomato
purée/concentrate

500 ml/2 cups olive oil

hot crumbed
prawns/shrimp

100 g/1 cup fresh
breadcrumbs

400 g/14 oz. king
prawns/jumbo shrimp,
uncooked

grated zest and freshly
squeezed juice of 2
unwaxed lemons

lemon wedges, to serve

sea salt

cocktail sticks/toothpicks

makes 40

hot crumbed prawns
with tomato aioli

Eat these lemon-drenched prawns/shrimp hot or cold
with sweet tomato aioli. Alternatively, you can thread
the prawns onto skewers and cook them on an outside
grill for a barbecue party.

Preheat the grill/broiler to high.

Put all the aioli ingredients, except the olive oil, in a food processor
and blend. With the motor running, gradually trickle in the oil, very
slowly at first, until you have a silky thick mayonnaise.

For the prawns/shrimp, lightly toast the breadcrumbs under the hot
grill/broiler until crisp and golden. Watch carefully and do not let
them burn. Combine the prawns/shrimp with the lemon zest and
half the lemon juice in a bowl. Transfer the prawns/shrimp to a
baking sheet and grill for 2–3 minutes, turning once, until they have
turned from blue to pink.

Quickly pile the prawns/shrimp onto a serving plate. Sprinkle the
remaining lemon juice over the prawns/shrimp, season with a little
sea salt and scatter the toasted breadcrumbs over the top. Serve
immediately with lemon wedges, cocktail sticks/toothpicks and the
tomato aioli for dipping.

swordfish souvlaki bites

2 swordfish steaks

sea salt and freshly ground black pepper

for the marinade

1 anchovy fillet, rinsed of oil

10 small capers

2 tablespoons fresh oregano, finely chopped or 1 teaspoon dried

1 garlic clove, finely chopped

3 tablespoons red wine vinegar

5 tablespoons extra-virgin olive oil

lemon wedges, to serve

12 wooden skewers, soaked in water for 30 minutes before use

a griddle pan/ridged stove-top grill pan

makes 12

Swordfish makes a great alternative to the usual chicken skewers. These souvlaki bites are inspired by Greek meze and so are full of Mediterranean flavours and particularly suited for summery gatherings as they are delicious cooked on the barbecue. If you can't find swordfish, tuna also works well.

Put all the ingredients for the marinade in a large bowl. Cut the swordfish into bite-sized cubes and add them to the bowl. Cover and refrigerate for 30 minutes, but no longer.

Thread two cubes of swordfish onto each skewer and season with salt and pepper. Heat a griddle/ridged stove-top grill pan or. Grill/broil the fish for 1–2 minutes on each side, until cooked through.

Serve warm, with a little of the marinade spooned over the top and lemon wedges on the side for squeezing.

spanish men

30 small Spanish olives, stoned

1 tablespoon extra virgin olive oil

1 tablespoon sherry vinegar

1 teaspoon smoked paprika (*pimentón*)

100 g/3½ oz. Serrano ham, thinly sliced

1 tablespoon very finely chopped fresh flat leaf parsley

150 g/5½ oz. membrillo (quince paste), cut into 30 identically-sized cubes

150 g/5½ oz. Manchego cheese, cut into 30 identically-sized cubes

cocktail sticks/toothpicks

makes 30

For maximum visual impact, present these in neat rows. Spanish Men can be assembled well in advance and kept chilled. Don't push the sticks all the way through the cheese, or the men won't stand up!

Begin by marinating the olives in the olive oil, sherry vinegar and smoked paprika for an hour or so.

Lay out the Serrano ham and rub the parsley over each slice. Cut into 30 equal-sized pieces (approximately 3 pieces from each slice). Roll up each small piece as tightly as possible into a cylinder and chill for 20 minutes.

Assemble the men by threading the components onto a cocktail stick/toothpick in the following order: an olive, a cube of membrillo, a roll of ham and a cube of Manchego.

warm halloumi bites

2 tablespoons olive oil

200 g/7 oz. halloumi
cheese, cut into
bite-sized pieces

2 tablespoons chopped
flat leaf parsley

lemon wedges, to serve

cocktail sticks/toothpicks

serves 4–6

Halloumi bites are a great vegetarian alternative if
you want to serve skewers. Sauté the cubes of cheese
to really bring out the flavour and serve with plenty
of parsley and lemon and cocktail sticks to pick with.

Heat the olive oil in a frying pan/skillet until very hot. Working in
batches, brown the pieces of halloumi on both sides. Remove them
from the pan/skillet with a slotted spoon and drain on kitchen paper
to soak up any excess oil. Sprinkle with parsley and serve warm with
lemon wedges for squeezing over the top.

piri piri mushrooms

Piri piri is a fiery Portugese condiment made from a combination of red chillies, olive oil and vinger. Beware, these little morsels are very hot!

Blend all the piri piri ingredients in a food processor until you have a smooth liquid.

For the mushrooms, gently heat the olive oil in a large saucepan, add the garlic, mushrooms and half the parsley and cook over a medium heat for 3–4 minutes. Turn up the heat, add the piri piri mixture and cook for a further 3–4 minutes, using a wooden spoon to stir the mushrooms and prevent them from sticking.

Scatter in the remaining parsley, stir, and serve straight away in a shallow dish with cocktail sticks/toothpicks on the side for spearing (just as you would if serving olives).

piri piri

2 large fresh red chillies

2 large garlic cloves

2 teaspoons sea salt crystals

2 teaspoons white wine vinegar

2 tablespoons olive oil

mushrooms

2 tablespoons olive oil

1 garlic clove, crushed

400 g/14 oz. baby button mushrooms

a handful of fresh flat leaf parsley, chopped

cocktail sticks/toothpicks

makes 30

breads & crackers

garlic and herb bread

3 garlic cloves, peeled and crushed

1 tablespoon butter, very soft

3 tablespoons olive oil

1 tablespoon chopped fresh flat leaf parsley

1 tablespoon chopped fresh basil leaves

4 ciabatta rolls, split in half

serves 8

This healthy but tasty recipe uses less butter than 'normal' garlic bread. They are delicious eaten on their own or served with salad as part of a buffet table.

Preheat the oven to 200°C (400°F) Gas 6.

Combine the garlic, butter, oil, parsley and basil in a bowl and whisk, mixing well, until the butter and oil emulsify.

Spread each half-roll generously with the butter, place the two halves together and wrap each roll in foil. Bake for 10–15 minutes.

If you are using a barbecue/outside grill, place the foil parcels over a medium heat for 10 minutes, turning once.

sage and stilton flatbread

Serve this with drinks when your guests arrive. If Stilton is not your favourite cheese, try using another blue cheese such as Roquefort or Gorgonzola, or try brie or a hard cheese, such as Cheddar.

500 g/5 cups plain/all-purpose flour

1 teaspoon baking powder

225 ml/1 scant cup Greek yoghurt

100 g/7 tablespoons butter, melted

2 eggs, beaten

3 tablespoons chopped fresh sage

100 g/3½ oz. Stilton cheese, crumbled

a baking sheet, lightly oiled

serves 8

Sift the flour and baking powder into a bowl and make a well in the centre. Put the yoghurt, melted butter, eggs and sage in a separate bowl and mix. Pour the yoghurt mixture into the well in the flour and stir with a wooden spoon until well blended.

Preheat the oven to 180°C (350°F) Gas 4.

Knead the dough into a ball, put on the oiled baking sheet and roll out to a circle about 30 cm/12 inch diameter. Bake in the preheated oven for 20 minutes. Remove the bread from the oven, crumble the Stilton over the top and return to the oven for a further 10 minutes. Remove the bread from the oven and let cool a little. Transfer to a large chopping board, cut into wedges and serve.

first phase dough

200 ml/¾ cup plus 1 tablespoon warm water

1½ teaspoons dried quick-acting yeast

130 g/1 cup strong/bread flour

second phase dough

1 tablespoon olive oil

1½ teaspoons salt

165 g/1¼ cups strong/bread flour

topping

250 ml/1 cup passata or strained tomatoes

2 tablespoons olive oil, plus extra to brush

1 tablespoon freshly chopped oregano, plus extra to decorate

½ teaspoon salt

¼ teaspoon crushed black pepper

150 g/5½ oz. mozzarella cheese, torn into pieces

40 g/¼ cup stoned black olives, chopped

2–3 non-stick baking sheets

makes 16

little margherita pizzas with olives

These fresh little pizzas are perfect to enjoy with a glass of wine and are guaranteed to be greeted with delight. And cooking them just before the guests arrive will fill your home with delicious welcoming smells.

To make the first phase dough, put the warm water and yeast in a mixing bowl and whisk, then add the flour and whisk again until well mixed. Cover and set aside in a warm place for 1 hour.

In the meantime, make the topping. Put the passata/strained tomatoes, oil, oregano, salt and pepper in a bowl, mix and set aside.

After 1 hour the first phase dough will be bubbly and have increased in size. For the second phase, add the oil, salt and flour and mix well to form a dough. Transfer to a well floured surface and knead for a few minutes. Divide the dough into 16 and roll each into a ball. Roll out with a rolling pin until you have a base roughly 10 cm/4 inches in diameter. Put the bases on the baking sheets and brush well with oil. Spread some of the tomato sauce over each base and top with mozzarella and olives. Let rest in a warm place for 30 minutes.

Preheat the oven to 200°C (400°F) Gas 6.

Bake in the preheated oven for about 12 minutes. Remove from the oven and scatter more oregano over the top. Leave to cool for a couple of minutes, then serve hot.

cheese straws

125 g/1 cup plain/all-purpose flour

a pinch of sea salt

½ teaspoon cayenne pepper

½ teaspoon mustard powder

100 g/6½ tablespoons unsalted butter, chilled and diced

100 g/1 cup mixed grated mature Cheddar and Parmesan cheese

a baking sheet, lined with baking parchment

makes about 24

Cheesy and just a little bit spicy, these straws are lovely enjoyed with a glass of Mulled Cider (see page 235).

Sift the flour, salt, cayenne and mustard powder into the bowl of a food processor. Add the butter and pulse the ingredients until they look like breadcrumbs. Add the grated cheeses and pulse again until the dough starts to come together into a ball.

To knead the dough, sprinkle a little flour onto a clean work surface. Shape the dough into a ball and push on it and press it onto the work surface. Do this very briefly, just to bring the dough together. Flatten into a disc, cover with clingfilm/plastic wrap and chill in the refrigerator for 30 minutes.

Preheat the oven to 190°C (375°F) Gas 5.

Tip the dough onto the floured work surface and roll out until it is about 6–7 mm/¼ inch thick. Cut into 1-cm/⅜-inch wide strips and arrange on the prepared baking sheet. Bake on the middle shelf of the preheated oven for about 12 minutes, or until golden. Serve warm or cold.

stilton and celery bites

140 g/1 cup plus
1 tablespoon plain/all-purpose flour

60 g/4 tablespoons
unsalted butter, chilled
and cubed

85 g/3 oz. Stilton or
other strong blue cheese

½ teaspoon salt

½ teaspoon bicarbonate
of soda/baking soda

1 teaspoon celery salt

2 baking sheets, lined with
baking parchment

makes about 30–40

Stilton and celery are a perfect pairing. For the best result, use a strong Stilton or other blue cheese.

Preheat the oven to 150°C (300°F) Gas 2.

Put the flour, butter, cheese, salt, bicarbonate of soda/baking soda and celery salt in a food processor and pulse until the mixture resembles crumbs. Add 2 teaspoons water and pulse until the mixture comes together into a dough.

Transfer the dough to a lightly floured surface. Roll into a log about 3 cm/1¼ inches in diameter, wrap in clingfilm/plastic wrap and refrigerate for about 1 hour.

Remove the dough from the refrigerator and unwrap it. Cut into discs about 1-cm/½-inch thick. Arrange the discs on the prepared baking sheets, spacing them slightly apart as they may spread when they are baking.

Bake in the preheated oven for about 20 minutes, or until pale gold. Remove from the oven and let cool. Store in an airtight container for up to 2 weeks.

anchovy wafers

125 g/1 cup plain/all-purpose flour

125 g/1 stick chilled butter, cut into small cubes

125 g/4½ oz. strong mature Cheddar cheese, grated

2 tablespoons chopped fresh sweet marjoram or 2 teaspoons dried oregano

100 g/3½ oz. anchovies in olive oil, drained and halved lengthways

freshly ground black pepper

2 baking sheets

makes 40

Ready-made salty snacks pall beside these crumbly, melt-on-the-tongue wafers. They deserve to be paired with well-chilled dry Champagne. If you serve these, balance them with something sour or sweet.

Sift the flour onto a clean work surface, make a well in the centre and add the butter, cheese, herbs and black pepper. With clean, cool fingers, rub together to form a soft, tacky dough. Scoop the dough up, with the aid of a spatula if necessary, and put it on a large piece of baking parchment. Mould the mixture into a flattish rectangle, wrap up in the parchment and chill for 1 hour in the refrigerator.

Preheat the oven to 200°C (400°F) Gas 6. Using a sharp knife, cut the dough (just as you would slice a loaf of bread) into thin wafers and arrange them on baking sheets, positioning them not too close together. Lay an anchovy half lengthways on each wafer and bake for 8 minutes until golden. Let cool on a wire rack before serving.

parmesan and rosemary wafers

These are a must for any good party. Everyone will be constantly nibbling, so make plenty. They can be made up to 2 days in advance but must be kept chilled in an airtight container.

2 sprigs of rosemary, leaves stripped and finely chopped

200 g/7 oz. Parmesan cheese, coarsely grated

2 baking sheets, lined with baking parchment

makes 24

Preheat the oven to 200°C (400°F) Gas 6.

Put the rosemary and Parmesan in a bowl and mix. Put teaspoons of the mixture in little heaps on the baking sheets and flatten out into circles. Make sure they are not too close because they will spread in the oven. Bake in the preheated oven for 8–10 minutes until golden. Remove from the oven and let cool. Gently peel off the paper and serve.

miso and parmesan palmiers

1 sheet of frozen ready-rolled puff pastry

2 tablespoons white miso paste

50 g/3 tablespoons unsalted butter, softened

30 g/1 oz. Parmesan cheese, finely grated

1 tablespoon toasted sesame seeds

a baking sheet lined with baking parchment

makes about 24

This recipe is a unique take on the classic crumbly puff pastry biscuit – and is delicious served with drinks. The extreme savouriness of both miso and Parmesan makes them a great flavour match.

Lay the pastry on a clean work surface and allow it to defrost just enough so that it can be unrolled without cracking.

Combine the miso and butter in a small bowl and spread about two-thirds of this mixture evenly over the pastry. Sprinkle two-thirds of the grated Parmesan over the top. Fold the pastry in half. Spread the remaining butter mixture on the pastry and sprinkle over the remaining cheese. Fold the pastry over again to make a long rectangle shape and gently press down on the pastry. Put the pastry on the prepared baking sheet and then into the freezer for 30 minutes so that it can be cut easily.

When you are ready to cook the palmiers, preheat the oven to 200°C (400°F) Gas 6.

Using a sharp knife, cut the pastry into 1-cm/½-inch wide slices. Put the slices, cut-side up, on the baking sheet, sprinkle over the sesame seeds and bake in the preheated oven for about 15 minutes, until puffed and golden. Serve while still warm.

grissini sticks with parma ham

These bites are so easy to make. Buy good quality ingredients at an Italian delicatessen: the grissini sticks will be skinny and crunchy, made with good flour in the traditional way, and the Parma ham/prosciutto can be sliced to order. Assemble these nibbles up to an hour in advance of your party.

12 very thin slices Parma ham/prosciutto

12 grissini (Italian breadsticks)

makes 12

Trim off the excess fat from the Parma ham/prosciutto and wrap a slice around the top half of each grissini. Arrange in glasses or on a large plate and serve.

buffet dishes

honeyed chicken wings

16 chicken wings

200 ml/¾ cup runny honey

100 ml/scant ½ cup sweet chilli sauce

sea salt and freshly ground black pepper

a bunch of radishes, trimmed, to serve (optional)

serves 8

These really should be called Last Lick Chicken Wings – anyone who eats them removes every morsel of flavour and sticky meat. Just watch out that they don't burn in the oven. They can be made the day before the party, just cover them and chill until needed.

Preheat the oven to 200°C (400°F) Gas 6.

Put the chicken wings in an oiled roasting tin. Cook them in the preheated oven for 40 minutes, turning them after 20 minutes so that they brown evenly.

Meanwhile, put the honey and sweet chilli sauce in a small saucepan. Season with salt and pepper to taste and bring to the boil. Pour the sauce over the chicken wings, mix well and let cool. Serve with radishes, if using.

finger-lickin' drumsticks

4 tablespoons
Worcestershire sauce

4 tablespoons tomato
ketchup

4 tablespoons dark
brown sugar

2 tablespoons American
or Dijon mustard

8 chicken drumsticks
or 16 chicken wings

serves 8

This is a perfect dish for a barbecue party. The marinade
in this recipe is also great for pork chops or spare ribs.

For the marinade and dipping sauce, combine the Worcestershire
sauce, ketchup, sugar and mustard in a bowl.

Put the chicken in an airtight plastic bag, pour in half the sauce,
shake the bag and seal the end. Refrigerate for at least 3 hours.

Preheat the oven to 220°C (425°F) Gas 7. Remove the chicken from
the bag and cook in a baking dish for about 35–40 minutes, turning
the pieces occasionally.

Pour the remaining sauce into a pan, add 125 ml/½ cup water and
bring to the boil for 5 minutes, then pour into a small dish. Remove
the chicken from the oven and cool slightly, then serve with the
sauce for dipping.

If you are using a barbecue/outside grill, scrape any excess marinade
off the chicken. Cook over direct heat for 40 minutes, turning
occasionally so they brown and cook evenly.

750 g/1 lb 10 oz. beef
fillet, from the thin end

2 tablespoons olive oil

175 g/6 oz. fine green
beans, trimmed

3 large hard-boiled eggs

20-cm/8-inch piece
cucumber, peeled and
cut into long wedges

250 g/9 oz. ripe
tomatoes, quartered

75 g/½ cup small
wrinkled black olives

a handful of fresh basil
leaves, torn

sea salt and freshly
ground black pepper

beef marinade

2 tablespoons freshly
squeezed lime juice

2 tablespoons olive oil

2 garlic cloves, crushed

sea salt and freshly
ground black pepper

Thai dressing

2 tablespoons fish sauce

3 tablespoons freshly
squeezed lime juice

2 tablespoons light soy
sauce

1 tablespoon sweet chilli
sauce

3 tablespoons chopped
fresh coriander/cilantro

serves 4

fillet of beef salad with thai dressing

This makes a beautiful centrepiece on a table – especially when arranged on a large platter. It needs nothing more than a cold noodle salad to transform it into a feast for a summer party. Everything can be prepared ahead (even the day before) to be assembled at the last moment.

To prepare the beef marinade, mix the lime juice, olive oil, garlic, salt and pepper in a non-metal dish. Add the beef and toss to coat. Cover and let marinate in the refrigerator for 1 hour.

To cook the beef, heat another 2 tablespoons olive oil in a heavy roasting tin or frying pan/skillet on top of the stove until smoking. Lift the beef out of the marinade, pat dry and sear well all over until nicely browned. Transfer to a preheated oven at 200°C (400°F) Gas 6 and roast for 15–18 minutes for medium rare. Remove from the oven and transfer the beef to a plate to cool.

To make the Thai dressing, put the fish sauce, lime juice, soy sauce, chilli sauce and coriander/cilantro in a bowl, whisk well, then set aside to infuse.

Bring a saucepan of salted water to the boil, add the beans and blanch for 4 minutes. Drain, refresh in cold water, then set aside.

Peel the eggs and cut them in quarters. Heat the dressing and keep it warm. Toss the beans, cucumber, tomatoes and olives with half the dressing and pile on a flat serving platter.

Cut the beef in slices and lay them on top of the vegetables. Dot the eggs all around, strew with the basil, spoon over the remaining dressing and grind pepper on top before serving.

1 large salmon, about 1.5 kg/3 lb 5 oz., scaled and gutted through the gills if possible

cucumber salad

2 large cucumbers

1 tablespoon sea salt

1 tablespoon sugar

100 ml/scant ½ cup white wine or cider vinegar

2 tablespoons chopped fresh dill

freshly ground white pepper

court bouillon

1.5 litres/6 cups water

1 tablespoon sea salt

150 ml/⅔ cup white wine

1 onion, sliced

2 celery sticks, sliced

1 carrot, sliced

a handful of fresh parsley stalks

2 bay leaves

1 teaspoon black peppercorns

to serve

extra chopped fresh dill

homemade mayonnaise

wasabi paste (optional)

a fish kettle or large roasting tin with a rack and foil

serves 6

whole poached salmon with sweet and sour pickled cucumber

There is something quite magnificent about serving a whole fish, simply decorated with pale green cucumber 'scales'. It is very impressive and so easy – this method of cooking the fish keeps it wonderfully moist, with no chance of overcooking or damaging the fish.

To make the cucumber salad, peel the cucumber and slice as thinly as possible with a mandoline or in a food processor. Spread in a colander and sprinkle with salt, mixing well. Stand the colander on a plate and leave to disgorge for 30 minutes. Rinse well and squeeze the excess moisture out of the cucumber. Spread the slices over a large plate. Dissolve the sugar in the vinegar and stir in the dill. Pour the mixture over the cucumber and let marinate for at least 1 hour. Grind over lots of white pepper before serving with the salmon.

Put all the court bouillon ingredients in a large saucepan, bring to the boil and simmer for 1 hour. Let cool completely, then strain the liquid into a fish kettle or large roasting tin. Carefully lower the salmon into the liquid (use the rack to do this). The liquid must cover the fish; if not, top up with a little water. On the stove top, bring slowly to the boil, then cover and turn off the heat. Let cool in the liquid. When completely cold, lift out and drain the fish, then remove the skin and slide onto a serving dish.

Cover the salmon with cucumber 'scales', serving any remaining cucumber separately. Sprinkle with dill and serve with thick homemade mayonnaise flavoured with a dash of Japanese wasabi paste, if using.

smoked trout, celeriac and apple salad

Here is a simple combination of ingredients that meld together to make a deliciously fresh-tasting salad. It's a salad in the slaw sense of the word and is best eaten spooned onto crisp little toasts.

200 g/7 oz. celeriac, peeled and grated

185 ml/¾ cup good-quality mayonnaise

1 tablespoon freshly squeezed lemon juice

1 smoked trout fillet, about 300 g/10 oz.

2 sweet eating apples, such as Red Delicious, cut into wedges

2 teaspoons finely chopped fresh tarragon

2 tablespoons finely chopped fresh flat leaf parsley

½ teaspoon smoked paprika (*pimentón*)

1 baguette, to serve

serves 4–6

Combine the celeriac, mayonnaise and lemon juice in a bowl.

Peel the skin from the trout and discard. Roughly flake the fish into a separate mixing bowl. Add the apple wedges, tarragon, parsley, paprika and the celeriac mixture. Gently toss to combine without breaking up the fish too much. Spoon into a serving bowl.

Preheat the grill/broiler. Finely slice the baguette. Toast on both sides until golden. Cut into triangles and serve alongside the salad.

375 g/13 oz. ready-rolled puff pastry

1 large or two smaller red bell peppers

1 large or two smaller yellow bell peppers

3 tablespoons olive oil

2 whole cloves of garlic, flattened

4 heaped tablespoons red pesto

150 g/5½ oz. buffalo mozzarella, drained and finely sliced

125 g/4½ oz. red cherry tomatoes, de-stalked and halved

125 g/4½ oz. yellow cherry tomatoes, de-stalked and halved

½ teaspoon dried oregano or marjoram

1 medium egg, lightly beaten

a little freshly grated Parmesan cheese

a few fresh basil leaves

sea salt and freshly ground black pepper

serves 4–6

heirloom tomato, pepper and mozzarella tart

This tart looks spectacular, but is so easy to prepare.

Preheat the oven to 200°C (400°F) Gas 6. Take the pastry out of the refrigerator at least 20 minutes before you need to unroll it.

Quarter the peppers, remove the pith and seeds and cut each quarter into half lengthways. Put them in a roasting tin with the garlic cloves, pour over 2 tablespoons olive oil, mix together well and roast for about 20–25 minutes until the edges of the peppers are beginning to blacken. Remove and cool for 10 minutes.

Unroll the pastry and lay on a lightly greased rectangular baking sheet. With a sharp knife score a line round the pastry 1¼ cm/½ inch from the edge. Spread the pesto evenly inside the rectangle you've marked. Lay the pepper strips across the base of the tart, alternating red and yellow sections. Tear the mozzarella slices roughly and distribute over the peppers. Grind over some black pepper. Arrange the halved tomatoes over the peppers, red on yellow and yellow on red. Rub the oregano or marjoram over the tart, season with a little salt and a little more pepper and trickle over the remaining oil.

Turn the oven heat up to 220°C (425°F) Gas 7. Brush the edges of the tart with the beaten egg and bake for 12 minutes or until the edge of the tart is well puffed up and beginning to brown. Turn the heat back down to 200°C (400°F) Gas 6 and cook for another 12–15 minutes until the tops of the tomatoes are well browned. Coarsely grate or shave a little Parmesan over the tart then let cool for 5 minutes. Tear the basil leaves roughly and scatter them over the tart. Serve warm.

375 g/13 oz. ready-made shortcrust pastry

75 g/5 tablespoons unsalted butter

1 onion, sliced

450 g/1 lb Portobello or other dark, open mushrooms, sliced

freshly squeezed juice of 1 lemon

2 tablespoons chopped fresh tarragon

200 g/7 oz. mascarpone cheese, softened

3 large eggs, beaten

sea salt and freshly ground black pepper

garlic crunch topping

50 g/4 tablespoons butter

150 g/1 cup stale breadcrumbs

3 garlic cloves, chopped

finely grated zest of 1 unwaxed lemon

3 tablespoons chopped fresh parsley

a deep, fluted tart tin, 25 cm/10 inch diameter

foil or baking parchment and baking beans

serves 6–8

portobello mushroom and tarragon tart

Large dark mushrooms, such as the Portobello variety, are full of flavour – the darker, the better. This tart has a creamy filling laced with tarragon and lemon. The garlicky crunchy topping turns it into a giant version of a stuffed mushroom – but more sophisticated!

Bring the pastry to room temperature. Preheat the oven to 200°C (400°F) Gas 6.

Roll out the pastry thinly on a lightly floured work surface. Use to line the tart tin, then chill or freeze for 15 minutes and bake blind following the method given on page 49.

Melt the butter in a frying pan/skillet, add the onion and fry until soft and golden. Add the mushrooms, lemon juice, salt and pepper, then fry over a medium heat for 5 minutes until the mushrooms are tender and the liquid has evaporated. Stir in the tarragon, then let the mixture cool slightly.

To make the topping, melt the butter in a frying pan/skillet, add the breadcrumbs, garlic, lemon zest and parsley and fry over brisk heat until the breadcrumbs begin to crisp but not colour too much. Tip the mixture into a bowl.

Put the mascarpone and eggs into a bowl and beat well. Stir in the mushroom mixture. Pour into the pastry case, then sprinkle with the topping and bake for 20–25 minutes until set, crisp and golden on top. Serve warm.

catalan chickpea salad

3 tablespoons extra
virgin olive oil

1 red onion, sliced

2 garlic cloves, chopped

200 g/7 oz. cured
chorizo, sliced

2 bay leaves, bruised

2 tablespoons pine nuts,
toasted in a dry frying
pan/skillet (optional)

400 g/2 cups canned
chickpeas, drained,
reserving 2 tablespoons
of liquid

coarsely ground black
pepper

1 small tomato, finely
chopped, to serve

serves 4

This delicious, warm salad relies on just a handful of ingredients. With such a wonderful combination of flavours, you would never guess that it has a cooking time of just five minutes – perfect for when you have other buffet dishes to prepare. You can forgo the pine nuts, but they do add a lovely bite to this salad.

Heat the oil in a frying pan/skillet, add the onion, garlic, chorizo, and bay leaves and fry over gentle heat for 5 minutes or until softened but not browned. Stir in the toasted pine nuts, if using, and chickpeas with their liquid. Heat until the flavours are combined, mashing a little with a fork.

Sprinkle with pepper and the chopped tomato and serve hot, warm, or cool, but never chilled.

grilled pepper, tomato and chilli salad

The gentle aromatic spicing of this Moroccan cooked salad is just perfect for a summer buffet. You can prepare it a few hours ahead and leave in the refrigerator for the flavours to develop.

2 medium-sized green bell peppers

3–4 long sweet peppers

400 g/14 oz. ripe tomatoes, skinned*

¼ teaspoon smoked sweet paprika (*pimentón dulce*)

¼ teaspoon ground cumin

1 tablespoon lemon juice

2 tablespoons olive oil

2 tablespoons pickled sliced Jalapeño chillies, rinsed and finely chopped

1 heaped tablespoon finely chopped fresh parsley

sea salt and freshly ground black pepper

serves 6

To peel the green and sweet peppers, either lay them over a low gas flame, turning frequently until the skins char, or halve them, lay them skin side upwards on a grill/broiler pan and grill/broil under a high heat until the skins are blackened. Put the charred peppers in a bowl and cover with clingfilm/plastic wrap (this helps to loosen the skins). Once the peppers are cool, rinse and rub them under cold running water, and the skins should slip off.

Deseed the peppers, slice them thickly and put in a serving bowl with the tomatoes. Measure the paprika and cumin into another small bowl and whisk in the lemon juice and oil. Season to taste with salt and pepper. Pour the dressing over the peppers, add the Jalepeños and parsley and toss together.

*To skin the tomatoes make a small cut near the stalk of each one with a sharp knife, put them in a bowl and pour over boiling water. Leave for a minute then pour the water away and cover the tomatoes with cold water. The skins should peel off easily.

250 g/9 oz. bulgur

50 g/2 oz. chopped, roasted hazelnuts

50 g/2 oz. shelled pistachios, roughly chopped

5–6 spring onions/scallions, trimmed and finely sliced

½ cucumber, peeled, deseeded and finely chopped

1 red ramiro pepper, halved, deseeded and finely chopped

3 medium-sized ripe tomatoes, skinned and finely chopped

1 medium pomegranate

freshly squeezed juice of 2 lemons (6 tablespoons)

½ teaspoon salt

1 teaspoon ground cumin

1 teaspoon chilli/hot red pepper flakes

3 tablespoons extra virgin olive oil

1 tablespoon pomegranate syrup or 2 teaspoons balsamic vinegar and 1 teaspoon sugar

5 tablespoons finely chopped fresh parsley

3 tablespoons finely chopped fresh mint leaves

3 tablespoons finely chopped fresh dill leaves

sea salt and freshly ground black pepper

serves 6

kisir

This Turkish recipe is the perfect party salad. It is so pretty and you can vary it depending on what you have available, substituting walnuts for hazelnuts or pistachios for example, adding some olives or some finely snipped dried apricots or replacing the dill with fresh coriander/cilantro.

Put the bulgur in a large bowl and pour over enough boiling water to just cover the grain. Leave for 15 minutes for the liquid to absorb then pour over plenty of cold water, swirl the grain around and tip the grain into a sieve. Squeeze the grain with your hands to extract any excess water and return the grain to the bowl.

Add the chopped nuts, sliced spring onions/scallions, and chopped cucumber, pepper and tomatoes (including the seeds and pulp). Halve the pomegranate and scoop out the seeds, reserving the juice and discarding the pith. Add the pomegranate seeds to the salad.

Whisk the lemon juice and reserved pomegranate juice with the salt, cumin and chilli/hot red pepper flakes, whisk in the olive oil and pomegranate syrup or balsamic vinegar and sugar and season with salt and pepper. Tip into the salad and mix well. Finally mix in the chopped herbs. Toss well together and check the seasoning adding more salt, pepper or lemon juice to taste.

Cover and set aside for at least an hour for the flavours to infuse before serving.

roasted potato salad

1 kg/2 lb 4 oz. small new or salad potatoes, unpeeled and scrubbed

125 ml/½ cup extra virgin olive oil

1 small red onion, finely chopped

25 g/1 oz. pitted black olives, finely chopped

1½ tablespoons capers, rinsed and drained

6 sun-dried tomatoes in oil, drained and chopped

5 tablespoons chopped fresh flat leaf parsley

1 tablespoon balsamic vinegar

sea salt and freshly ground black pepper

serves 4–6

Though creamy mayonnaise-style sauces are traditional dressings for cold potato salads, highly flavoured dressings based on extra virgin olive oil have become popular. This salad is delicious served warm or cold.

Preheat the oven to 200°C (400°F) Gas 6.

Put the potatoes in a roasting tin, add 2 tablespoons of olive oil, sprinkle with salt and toss well to coat. Cook in the preheated oven for 25–30 minutes, or until tender, turning the potatoes from time to time so that they brown evenly.

Meanwhile, put all the remaining ingredients in a large bowl, mix well and season with salt and pepper.

Remove the potatoes from the oven, crush each potato slightly with a fork and cut in half. Toss the potatoes well in the bowl of dressing while they are still warm. Serve either warm or cold.

fruity coleslaw

A delicious fruity twist on a classic salad recipe. Using a food processor with a coarse grater will cut out the lengthy process of hand-grating. You can make it in advance of the party as it will keep in the refrigerator for a couple of days.

Combine the grated cabbage and carrot in a large bowl with the celery, apple and mango. Add the mayonnaise and season. Toss well to mix. Cover and leave in a cool place for 2–3 hours before serving.

350 g/12 oz. white or red cabbage, coarsely grated

1 large carrot, coarsely grated

2–3 celery sticks, finely sliced

1 red dessert apple, cored and diced

1 ripe mango, peeled and diced

150 ml/⅔ cup mayonnaise

sea salt and freshly ground black pepper

serves 8

raw vegetable platter

A selection of fresh vegetables makes a stunning centrepiece. Serve with just the olive oil and vinegar for dipping, or you could also try some of the dips from Chapter 1, such as the Crumbled Cheese Dip with Herbs and Pomegranate Seeds (page 20), or the Roasted Red Pepper and Walnut Dip (page 27).

8 carrots, cut into batons

8 baby fennel bulbs, trimmed and halved

1 cucumber, cut into batons

2 bunches of radishes, trimmed

8 tablespoons extra virgin olive oil

3 tablespoons balsamic vinegar

serves 12

Arrange the raw vegetables on a big serving plate. Put the oil and vinegar in a small dipping bowl and mix. Serve with the vegetables.

Ingredients

675 g/4 cups dried butter/lima beans

500 g/1 lb 2 oz. smoked Italian pancetta, fat/slab bacon or belly pork, in a piece

4 tablespoons olive oil

4 boneless duck breasts, halved crossways, or chicken legs or thighs

750 g/1 lb 10 oz. fresh Toulouse sausages or Italian coarse pork sausages, cut into 3 pieces each

2 medium onions, chopped

1 large carrot, chopped

4–6 large garlic cloves, crushed

3 bay leaves

2 teaspoons dried thyme

2 whole cloves

3 tablespoons tomato purée/concentrate

12 sun-dried tomatoes in oil, drained and coarsely chopped

75 g/1½ cups fresh white breadcrumbs (ciabatta is good too)

50 g/4 tablespoons butter

sea salt and freshly ground black pepper

serves 6–8

a big pot of cassoulet

This hearty dish from south-west France is big and filling, and great for large gatherings on cold winter days. It is traditionally made with a type of haricot bean, but this version uses butter/lima beans for their creamy texture, although any white bean can be substituted. All the components of the dish can be made days in advance, then assembled on the day. It reheats very well (top up with a little more liquid if it looks dry) and is a boon for entertaining vast numbers without fuss.

The night before, put the beans in a very large bowl, cover with plenty of cold water (to cover them by their depth again) and let soak for several hours.

The next day, drain the beans well and tip into a large saucepan. Cover with fresh water, bring to the boil, then simmer for about 1 hour or until just cooked. Drain well (reserving the cooking liquid).

Trim and discard the rind from the pancetta, and cut the flesh into large pieces. Heat 2 tablespoons of the oil in a frying pan/skillet, brown the pieces in batches and transfer to a plate. Heat the remaining oil in the pan, add the duck breasts and fry skin side down until the skin is golden. Transfer to the same plate as the pancetta. Brown the sausages in the same way and add to the plate. Add the onions to the pan, then the carrot, garlic, bay leaves, dried thyme, cloves, tomato purée/concentrate and sun-dried tomatoes. Cook for 5 minutes until softening.

To assemble the dish, put half the beans in a large, deep casserole. Add an even layer of all the meats, then the onion and tomato mixture. Season well with salt and pepper. Cover with the remaining beans, then add enough reserved hot cooking liquid until the beans are almost covered. Sprinkle evenly with the breadcrumbs and dot with butter. Bake the cassoulet in a preheated oven at 180°C (350°F) Gas 4 for about 1 hour until a golden crust has formed. Serve warm straight out of the dish.

about 12 sheets dried lasagne verdi

50 g/½ cup freshly grated Parmesan cheese

ragù

50 g/4 tablespoons butter

75 g/3 oz. pancetta or dry-cure smoked bacon in a piece, cubed

1 onion, finely chopped

1 carrot, chopped

1 celery stick, trimmed and finely chopped

250 g/9 oz. lean minced/ground beef

2 tablespoons tomato purée/concentrate

100 ml/⅓ cup dry white wine

200 ml/¾ cup beef stock or water

freshly grated nutmeg

sea salt and freshly ground black pepper

salsa besciamella

150 g/1¼ sticks butter

110 g/1 cup plain/all-purpose white flour

about 1 litre/4 cups milk

sea salt

a deep baking dish, about 20 x 25 cm/8 x 10 inches, buttered

serves 4–6

lasagne al forno

Lasagne is a great buffet option as it is very easy to assemble. Make the ragù the day before, and the *besciamella* on the day. Make sure the meat sauce is quite liquid as this will be absorbed into the pasta.

To make the ragù, melt the butter in a saucepan, add the cubed pancetta and cook for 2–3 minutes until browning. Add the onion, carrot and celery and brown these too. Stir in the minced beef and brown until just changing colour, but not hardening – break it up with a wooden spoon. Add the tomato purée/concentrate, mix well and pour in the wine and stock. Season well with grated nutmeg, salt and pepper. Bring to the boil, cover and simmer very gently for as long as you can – 2 hours if possible.

To make the besciamella, melt the butter in a medium saucepan. When foaming, add the flour and cook over gentle heat for about 5 minutes without letting it brown. Have a balloon whisk ready. Turn off the heat and add all the milk at once, whisking very well. When all the flour and butter have been amalgamated and there are no lumps, return to the heat and slowly bring to the boil, whisking all the time. When it comes to the boil, add salt, simmer gently for 2–3 minutes. Cover the surface directly with clingfilm/plastic wrap to prevent a skin forming.

Cook the sheets of dried lasagne in a large saucepan of boiling water in batches according to the packet instructions. Lift out with a slotted spoon and drain on a clean tea towel.

Preheat the oven to 180°C (350°F) Gas 4. Spoon one-third of the ragù into the buttered baking dish. Cover with 4 sheets of lasagne and spread with one-third of the besciamella. Repeat twice more, finishing with a layer of besciamella covering the whole top. Sprinkle with Parmesan cheese. Bake in the preheated oven for about 45 minutes, until brown and bubbling. Let stand for 10 minutes to settle and firm up before serving.

3 x 250 g/9 oz.
Camembert cheeses
in boxes

3 tablespoons Calvados
or brandy

3 tablespoons dark
chestnut honey

1 fat garlic clove, sliced

3 fresh sage leaves

3 sprigs fresh rosemary

3 fresh bay leaves

to serve

celery sticks

walnut bread

chilled French breakfast
radishes

serves about 15

trio of honey-baked camembert with calvados and herbs

This molten cheese dish is spiked with perfumed honey, pungent Calvados and garlic. Serve with crunchy celery sticks, warm crusty walnut bread and chilled radishes.

Preheat the oven to 200°C (400°F) Gas 6.

Unwrap the cheeses and return them to their boxes. Using a skewer, make 6 or 7 holes in each cheese. Mix the calvados and honey together and spoon the mixture into and over the holes. Stud with the garlic slices and lightly press the sage, rosemary and bay onto each cheese. Bake for about 7 minutes.

Remove the boxes from the oven. Using sharp scissors, quickly make 3 cuts on the surface of each cheese, from the centre out, and gently open the 'petals' a little. Take the cheeses out of their boxes, put them on a plate and serve straight away.

sweet treats

mini meringues brushed with bitter chocolate

Elegant clouds of meringue brushed with rich bitter chocolate. When the chocolate has set, gently smudge edible glitter (available from cake supply stores) over the chocolate to catch the light and sparkle.

3 egg whites

¼ teaspoon cream of tartar

175 g/¾ cup plus 2 tablespoons caster/superfine sugar

200 g/7 oz. bitter dark chocolate (60–70% cocoa solids), broken into small pieces

gold edible paint or edible glitter (optional)

a piping bag with fluted nozzle/tip

2 baking sheets lined with baking parchment

a soft pastry brush

makes 40–50

Preheat the oven to 130°C (250°F) Gas ½.

Put the egg whites in a clean, grease-free bowl and beat with an electric whisk until stiff. Add the cream of tartar and beat again. Very slowly add the sugar, beating constantly, until all the sugar is incorporated and you have a thick, glossy, silky mixture.

Fill a piping bag fitted with a fluted nozzle/tip with the mixture and pipe little 'tongues', each about 7 cm/3 inches long, onto a baking sheet lined with baking parchment. Bake for 30 minutes, then turn the oven temperature down to 110°C (225°F) Gas ¼ and continue baking for a further 2 hours until the meringues are dry.

When you are ready to decorate the meringues, put them on a wire rack. Set a heatproof bowl over a pan filled with boiling water, making sure the bowl does not touch the water. Put the chocolate in the bowl and leave to melt slowly. When it has melted, gently brush a lick of dark chocolate down the length of each meringue using a soft pastry brush. Leave to cool and set, then smudge on a little gold edible paint, if liked. Serve on a glass dish for impact.

raspberry and brown sugar meringues

In the middle of these meringues are wonderful little surprise explosions of fruit. They won't keep as long as conventional meringues, though, so serve them within a couple of hours of making them.

4 large fresh egg whites at room temperature

150 g/¼ cup caster/superfine sugar

50 g/¼ cup light brown muscovado sugar, sieved

200 g/1½ cups frozen raspberries, unthawed

2 large non-stick baking sheets, lightly greased with flavourless oil or a baking sheet lined with baking parchment

makes 16

Preheat the oven to 150°C (300°F) Gas 2.

Place the egg whites in a large clean greasefree bowl and start to whisk them (easiest with a hand-held electric whisk). Increase the speed as they begin to froth up, moving the whisk round the bowl, until they just hold a peak (about 2–3 minutes). Gradually add the caster/superfine sugar teaspoon by teaspoon beating the meringue well between each addition. When half the sugar has been incorporated, add the rest of the sugar a dessertspoon at a time. Gradually add in the brown sugar, then gently fold in the frozen raspberries ensuring they are fully coated by the meringue.

Using two dessertspoons, spoon the meringues onto the baking sheets. Place in the oven and immediately reduce the heat to 140°C (275°F) Gas 1 and bake for 1¼ hours until the meringue is firm. Turn off the heat and leave the meringues to cool in the oven. When they are cold, place them on a serving dish in a single layer so the juice doesn't run onto the meringues underneath. You can refrigerate them for up to three hours, lightly covered with clingfilm/plastic wrap, before serving.

praline and coffee éclairs

50 g/¼ cup granulated sugar

50 g/⅓ cup blanched hazelnuts, chopped

75 g/½ cup plus 1 tablespoon plain/all-purpose flour

60 ml/¼ cup milk

60 ml/¼ cup water

50 g/3 tablespoons butter, diced

a pinch of salt

2 eggs

125 ml/½ cup whipping cream

coffee icing

25 g/2 tablespoons unsalted butter

1 teaspoon instant coffee, dissolved in 3 tablespoons boiling water

200 g/1⅓ cups icing/confectioner's sugar, sifted

3 baking sheets, 1 lightly greased and 2 lined with baking parchment

a piping bag fitted with a 1–1.5-cm/½–¾-inch round nozzle/tip

makes about 20

French pâtisserie is the perfect treat for an afternoon tea party, and these baby éclairs look divine piled up on an elegant cake stand.

First make the praline. Heat the sugar in a dry saucepan over medium heat, stirring, for about 5 minutes until dissolved and pale gold. Add the hazelnuts and cook, stirring, for about 1 minute, then pour onto the greased baking sheet and let harden for at least 20 minutes.

Preheat the oven to 220°C (425°F) Gas 7.

Sift the flour onto a sheet of greaseproof/waxed paper. Heat the milk, water, butter and salt in a saucepan and bring to the boil for 1 minute. Remove from the heat and, stirring, add the flour to the pan. When the mixture becomes smooth, return to the heat, stirring constantly, for about 1 minute. Remove from the heat again and beat in the eggs, one at a time, until the mixture is smooth and glossy.

Spoon the mixture into the piping bag and pipe 5-cm/2-inch fingers of the mixture onto the lined baking sheets. Bake in the preheated oven for about 12 minutes until golden. Transfer to a wire rack and cut a slit in the side of each one. Let cool completely.

To make the filling, put the hardened praline in a food processor and process briefly to crush. Whip the cream until stiff, then fold in the crushed praline. Using the piping bag, fill the éclairs with the cream.

To make the coffee icing, put the butter and dissolved coffee in a heatproof bowl and set over a saucepan of simmering water until melted. Add the icing/confectioner's sugar and stir for about 4 minutes until smooth and glossy. Spoon the icing over the éclairs immediately and serve.

italian chocolate truffles

150 g/5½ oz. bitter dark chocolate (60–70% cocoa solids)

100 g/7 tablespoons salted butter, cubed

1 egg yolk

2 tablespoons Mozart Black Chocolate Liqueur or dark Crème de Cacao

1 teaspoon truffle honey or a drop of real truffle oil (optional)

unsweetened cocoa powder, to dust

a baking sheet, lined with baking parchment

makes about 15

This is a classic truffle recipe – very rich and dense, and reliant on the best-quality chocolate that you can find. For real truffle addicts, stir a little truffle honey or a drop of real truffle oil into the mixture – the flavour combination is quite mysterious but delicious!

Finely chop the chocolate and put it in a heat-proof bowl. Set the bowl over a pan of simmering water, making sure the bowl does not touch the water. Leave the chocolate to melt slowly.

When completely melted, beat in the butter, then the egg yolk, liqueur and truffle honey, if using. Cover with clingfilm/plastic wrap and refrigerate for about 1 hour, or until set.

Sift some cocoa powder onto a plate or into a bowl. Using two teaspoons, scoop the chilled chocolate mixture into rough mounds and put them on the prepared baking sheet. Shape each one into a knobbly truffle shape in your hands. Drop into the cocoa and roll each one around until it is completely covered then return to the baking sheet. If not serving immediately, layer in an airtight container between sheets of greaseproof/waxed paper and refrigerate for up to 5 days or freeze for up to 1 month.

white chocolate and lemon truffle balls

100 g/3½ oz. white chocolate

50 g/3 tablespoons butter

2 tablespoons double/heavy cream

¾ teaspoon grated lemon zest

115 g/4 oz. Madeira cake/pound cake, finely crumbled

to decorate

50 g/2 oz. white chocolate

icing/confectioner's sugar, for dusting

mini muffin or petit four cases

makes about 14

These buttery truffle balls flavoured with lemon zest are a lovely treat. They can be made in advance and chilled until ready to serve.

Break the white chocolate into a heatproof bowl, add the butter and set over a pan of gently simmering water until melted. Remove from the heat, add the cream and stir until the mixture is smooth and creamy. Then stir in the lemon zest, follwed by the cake crumbs.

Take spoonfuls of the mixture and use your fingers to roll them into walnut-sized balls. Place the balls in the paper cases and chill for at least 2 hours, until firm.

To decorate, melt the remaining chocolate in a bowl set over a pan of gently simmering water. Dip a skewer into the melted chocolate and drizzle zigzags of chocolate over the truffle balls. Chill until the chocolate has set. Dust lightly with icing/confectioner's sugar just before serving.

rose marzipan dates

Let your guests luxuriate in the delicate, subtle character of these romantic flavours. As well as toasted almonds, try decorating the dates with fresh edible roses, dried rosebuds or crystallized roses, or rolling them in sugar.

25 plump fresh dates

200 g/1⅓ cups ground almonds

100 g/⅔ cup icing/confectioner's sugar, sifted

freshly squeezed lemon juice

2 tablespoons rosewater

to decorate

caster/superfine sugar

freshly toasted flaked/slivered almonds, chopped

fresh rose petals, dried rosebuds or crystallized roses

makes 25

Slit the dates open lengthways and remove the stones. Put the ground almonds and icing/confectioner's sugar in a large bowl. Make a well in the centre and add a little lemon juice and the rosewater. Gradually combine the dry and wet ingredients, using a cold fork to work the mixture into a firm paste. It may appear initially that there is not enough moisture, but eventually the almonds will release their natural oils.

Divide the marzipan equally between the dates and decorate as desired.

chocolate-dipped strawberries

Chocolate always makes a sensational dessert but in this fun party snack it is balanced with fruit, in this case strawberries. Any variety of fruit can, of course, be dipped. These can be made up to 2 hours in advance.

100 g/3½ oz. dark chocolate

100 g/3½ oz. white chocolate

12 large strawberries

12 wooden skewers

serves 12

Put the dark chocolate and white chocolate in 2 separate bowls and set the bowls over 2 saucepans of simmering water. When melted, dip the pointed end of each strawberry into one of the chocolates and transfer to a sheet of baking parchment. When the chocolate is set, slide each strawberry onto a skewer and serve.

strawberry tartlets

3 tablespoons ground almonds

100 g/¾ cup plain/all-purpose flour

1 tablespoon sugar

50 g/3 tablespoons chilled butter, cubed

100 ml/scant ½ cup fresh ready-made custard/prepared pastry cream

200 g/7 oz. strawberries

icing/confectioner's sugar, for dusting

a 12-hole mini tartlet tin, greased

a plain cookie cutter, 6.5 cm/2½ inch diameter

makes 12

These pretty little tartlets look impressive but are very easy to make. You can cheat and use ready-made fresh custard for the filling so that the only cooking that's required is making the crisp almond pastry cases. Tiny wild strawberries are perfect, but if you can't find any, simply use slices of large strawberries.

Put the ground almonds, flour and sugar in a food processor and pulse to combine. Add the butter and pulse again until the mixture resembles fine breadcrumbs. With the motor still running, gradually add 2 tablespoons water until the mixture comes together to form a dough. Wrap in clingfilm/plastic wrap and chill in the refrigerator for at least 30 minutes.

Preheat the oven to 190°C (375°F) Gas 5.

Roll out the pastry thinly and stamp out 12 rounds using a cookie cutter. Press the rounds into the tartlet tin and prick the bases with a fork. Bake for about 12 minutes until crisp and golden. Remove from the oven, transfer to a wire rack and let cool.

To assemble, carefully spoon a little custard/pastry cream into the bottom of each tartlet case, top with a slice of strawberry and dust with a little icing/confectioner's sugar to serve.

ginger and chilli caramel cookies

50 g/3 tablespoons unsalted butter, at room temperature

100 g/½ cup sugar (golden caster/superfine, if available)

1 egg

50 g/½ cup crystallized ginger, finely chopped

130 g/1 cup plain/all-purpose flour

1½ teaspoons baking powder

2 teaspoons ground ginger

chilli caramel

100 g/½ cup sugar (golden caster/superfine, if available)

a pinch of ground cayenne pepper or hot chilli powder (or more if you like the heat!)

1–2 baking sheets, lined with baking parchment

makes about 15

These addictive cookies make a real talking point at parties! With a generous dose of crystallized ginger and bit of chilli heat, they are not for the faint-hearted.

Preheat the oven to 160°C (325°F) Gas 3.

Cream the butter and sugar in a mixing bowl until light and fluffy. Add the egg and mix well, then stir in the crystallized ginger. Mix the flour, baking powder and ground ginger in a separate bowl, then gently fold into the wet ingredients.

Take a generous teaspoon of the dough and place on one of the prepared baking sheets. Flatten it slightly, then repeat this process with the remaining dough, spacing the dough balls well apart as they will spread when they are baking.

Bake in the preheated oven for about 25 minutes, or until the biscuits are golden. Remove from the oven and leave to cool while you make the chilli caramel.

To make the chilli caramel, put the sugar in a heavy-based saucepan over medium heat. The sugar can burn quite easily (which can render the caramel bitter), so stir it often and keep a close eye on it. After a few minutes, the sugar should have completely melted. Remove from the heat and stir in the pepper or chilli powder. Be very careful when handling caramel as it can easily burn you. Use it immediately before it starts to harden.

Using a spoon, drizzle the caramel over the cookies any way you like. The caramel sets extremely quickly. When it has set, remove the cookies from the tray. Store in an airtight container for up to 1 week, but be warned that the caramel can seep into the biscuits in particularly humid conditions.

plum pastries

You don't have to use plums and almonds to fill these easy pastries, you can use any of your favourite fruit and nuts. They can be made up to 6 hours in advance.

2 sheets ready-made puff pastry

12 plums, halved and pitted

8 teaspoons honey

2 tablespoons flaked/slivered almonds

2 baking sheets, lightly oiled

makes 12

Preheat the oven to 180°C (350°F) Gas 4.

Cut each sheet of pastry in half lengthways to give 4 pieces of pastry. Cut each piece of pastry crossways to make 3 rectangles each, there should be 12 in total.

Put 2 plum halves on each piece of pastry, then sprinkle with the honey and almonds.

Bake in the preheated oven for 15–20 minutes until puffed and golden. Remove from the oven and serve warm or cold.

pastry

250 g/2 cups
plain/all-purpose flour,
plus extra for dusting

125 g/1 stick chilled
butter, cut into cubes

75 g/½ cup icing/
confectioner's sugar

1 egg

seeds from ½ vanilla pod

1 tablespoon Calvados

fresh walnut halves, to
decorate (optional)

milk, to glaze

icing/confectioner's
sugar, for dredging

filling

750 g/1 lb 10 oz. eating
apples, peeled, cored
and finely chopped or
roughly grated

100 ml/3½ oz. Calvados

150 g/¾ cup muscovado/
raw cane sugar

75 g/5 tablespoons
butter

seeds from ½ vanilla pod

6 cm/2½ inch and
5 cm/2 inch plain cookie
cutters

2 x 12-hole mini muffin
tins

makes 24

apple and calvados pies

These pies, made with French apple brandy, are delicious served with gooey cheeses, as an alternative to mince pies, or with a big bowl of whipped cream. You can also introduce a little variation by replacing some of the lids with a fresh walnut half.

First make the pastry. Put the flour, butter and icing/confectioner's sugar in a food processor and process until the mixture resembles fine breadcrumbs. Mix the egg with the vanilla seeds and Calvados and add to the mixture. Process quickly until it forms a lump of dough, then wrap in clingfilm/plastic wrap and chill in the refrigerator for 30 minutes.

Preheat the oven to 200°C (400°F) Gas 6.

To prepare the filling, put the apples in a bowl and splash the Calvados over the top. Leave to stand for 10 minutes. Put the apples in a heavy-based saucepan with the sugar, butter and vanilla seeds and set over medium heat. Cook until the apples are tender and the liquid has evaporated, stirring occasionally.

Lightly flour a work surface and roll out the chilled pastry carefully. You might have to do this in 2 batches. Stamp out 24 rounds using a 6-cm/2½-inch plain cookie cutter and use them to line the mini muffin tins. Using a teaspoon, fill the pies with the apple filling; pack them quite full, but do not heap. Stamp out the remaining pastry using a 5-cm/2-inch plain cookie cutter and press lightly onto the pies. Brush sparingly with milk and bake for 20–25 minutes. Cool on a wire rack and dredge with icing/confectioner's sugar to serve.

mince pies

Your guests will find these delicious mince pies hard to resist. Serve them warm from the oven, on their own or with a dollop of whipped cream or brandy butter. To give the pies an extra Christmassy feel, cut the pastry lids into star shapes using a star-shaped cutter, rather than rounds.

225 g/1½ cups plain/all-purpose flour

a pinch of salt

115 g/1 stick butter, chilled and diced

3–4 tablespoons cold water

225 g/8 oz. mincemeat

milk, for brushing

granulated sugar, for sprinkling

whipped cream or brandy butter, to serve

a fluted cookie cutter, 7.5 cm/3 inch diameter

a fluted cookie cutter, 6 cm/2½ inch diameter

a 12-hole tartlet tin, greased

makes 12

Sift the flour and salt into a bowl and add the butter. Using your fingertips, lightly rub the butter into the flour until the mixture resembles fine breadcrumbs. Gradually add the water, stirring with a blunt knife or a palette knife, until the mixture begins to come together in large lumps. Add a little extra water, if necessary.

Alternatively, put the flour, salt and butter in a food processor and process until the mixture resembles fine breadcrumbs. Add the water and process briefly until the mixture just comes together in a ball.

Collect the dough together and knead it gently, very briefly, on a lightly floured surface. Wrap in clingfilm/plastic wrap and chill in the refrigerator for 30 minutes.

Preheat the oven to 190°C (375°F) Gas 5.

On a lightly floured surface, roll out just over half the pastry and stamp out 12 circles of pastry using the larger cutter. Gently press these pastry circles into the tartlet tin. Divide the mincemeat evenly between the pastry cases.

Roll out the remaining pastry and stamp out 12 pastry circles using the smaller cutter. Dampen the edges of the pastry circles with water, then place them on top of the mincemeat and pastry in the tartlet tin, dampened edges down. Press the edges together to seal. Brush the tops of the pies with a little milk, then sprinkle with sugar. Using a sharp knife, cut a slit in the top of each pie. Bake in a preheated oven for 20–25 minutes, or until the pastry is cooked and lightly browned.

Remove from the oven and leave the mince pies in the tin for a couple of minutes, then transfer to a wire rack to cool. Serve warm.

sparkly tiara cupcakes

115 g/1 stick butter,
at room temperature

115 g/generous ½ cup
sugar

2 eggs

115 g/¾ cup self-raising
flour

1 teaspoon pure vanilla
extract

2 tablespoons whole milk

to decorate

about 6 clear red boiled
sweets/candies

185 g/1¼ cups
icing/confectioner's
sugar, sifted

1 egg white

lilac food colouring

edible sparkles and
edible silver balls

a 12-hole cupcake tin,
lined with plain or
patterned paper cases

makes 12

These are the ultimate cupcakes for princesses
everywhere, and are perfect for all sorts of occasions,
from birthday parties to hen parties!

Preheat the oven to 180°C (350°F) Gas 4. Put the butter and sugar
in a large bowl and beat until pale and fluffy. Beat in the eggs, one
at a time. Sift over the flour and fold in, then fold in the vanilla
extract and milk. Spoon the mixture into the paper cases, then bake
for about 17 minutes, until risen and golden and a skewer inserted
in the centre of a cupcake comes out clean. Transfer to a wire rack
and let cool completely before decorating.

To decorate, leave the sweets/candies in their wrappers and tap with
a rolling pin to break into large pieces. Set aside. To make the icing,
gradually beat the icing/confectioner's sugar into the egg white until
smooth and creamy, then beat in a few drops of food colouring until
the desired colour has been achieved. Spread the icing on top of the
cakes. Pile a little heap of boiled sweet/candy 'jewels' in the centre
of each cake and sprinkle with edible sparkles and silver balls.
Let set slightly before serving.

100 g/⅔ cup walnut or pecan pieces

175 g/1½ sticks unsalted butter

250 g/9 oz. dark bittersweet chocolate, chopped

1¼ cups sugar

3 eggs

1 teaspoon vanilla extract

150 g/1 cup plus 2 tablespoons plain/all-purpose flour

a pinch of salt

red and green sweets/candies, to decorate

edible Christmas sprinkles, to decorate

chocolate frosting

175 g/6 oz. bitter dark chocolate, chopped

125 g/1 stick unsalted butter, diced

125 ml/½ cup milk

1 teaspoon vanilla extract

225 g/1¾ cups icing/confectioner's sugar

a 23-cm/9-inch square baking tin, greased and lined with baking parchment

makes 16

frosted brownie squares

Scrumptious, deep, chocolatey brownies that are topped with a delicious chocolate buttercream and scattered with festive candies are party treats that will be appreciated by guests of all ages.

Preheat the oven to 180°C (350°F) Gas 4.

Put the walnuts or pecans on a baking sheet and roast them for 5 minutes in the preheated oven. Let them cool.

Put the butter and chocolate in a heatproof bowl over a pan of simmering water, not letting the bowl touch the water. Stir very carefully until it has melted, then let cool slightly.

Put the sugar and eggs in a mixing bowl and beat with an electric whisk until pale and thick. Add the vanilla and chocolate mixture and mix well.

Sift the flour and salt into the mixing bowl and fold in using a large metal spoon or spatula. Add the nuts and stir to combine. Pour the batter into the prepared baking tin. Bake in the preheated oven for about 30 minutes.

To make the frosting, put the butter and chocolate in a heatproof bowl over a pan of simmering water, not letting the bowl touch the water. Stir very carefully until it has melted.

Put the milk, vanilla extract and sugar in a mixing bowl and stir until smooth. Pour the melted chocolate into the mixing bowl and stir until smooth and thickened. You may need to leave this somewhere cool for 30 minutes to thicken enough to spread.

When the brownies have cooled, spread the chocolate frosting evenly over the them. Scatter the sweets/candies and sprinkles over the top, cut into squares, and serve.

50 g/3 tablespoons butter

50 g/¼ cup caster/superfine sugar

3 tablespoons double/heavy cream

25 g/3 tablespoons flaked/slivered almonds

75 g/½ cup mixed nuts, roughly chopped

4 glacé cherries, roughly chopped

40 g/¼ cup mixed peel, roughly chopped

15 g/2 tablespoons dried cranberries

25 g/3 tablespoons plain/all-purpose flour

100 g/3½ oz. white chocolate, broken into small pieces

2 baking sheets, lined with baking parchment and greased

makes about 24

white chocolate and cranberry florentines

Perfect little bites for an afternoon tea party, just the right size for balancing on a saucer!

Preheat the oven to 180°C (350°F) Gas 4. Put the butter, sugar and cream in a saucepan and set over low heat. Gently stir until melted, then bring to the boil. Remove from the heat and stir in the nuts, glacé cherries, mixed peel, cranberries and flour, and mix to combine. Drop teaspoonfuls of the mixture on the prepared baking sheets, spacing them well apart. Bake in the preheated oven for about 10 minutes until golden, then remove from the oven and gently press the edges, using a palette knife, to form neat rounds. Leave to cool on the baking sheets for about 10 minutes until firm, then carefully peel off the baking parchment and transfer the florentines to a wire rack to cool completely.

Put the white chocolate in a heatproof bowl and set it over a pan of simmering water. Stir it as it melts and let cool. Spread the underside of each florentine with a layer of white chocolate, then leave to firm up slightly before using the tines of a fork to make wavy lines in the chocolate. Leave to set.

spiced star cookies

125 g/1 stick unsalted butter, at room temperature

125 g/⅔ cup sugar

125 g/½ cup golden/corn syrup

1 egg

1 teaspoon ground ginger

400 g/3 cups self-raising flour

125 g/¾ cup icing/confectioner's sugar, sifted

4–5 teaspoons freshly squeezed lemon juice

edible silver balls, to decorate

2 baking sheets, lightly greased

star-shaped cookie cutters of various sizes

makes about 30

Nothing says Christmas like the smell of these cookies. They are an irresistible seasonal treat to serve with a glass of mulled wine or cider.

Put the butter and sugar in a large bowl and beat until light and fluffy. Add the golden/corn syrup, egg and ginger and beat again until well combined. Gradually sift in the flour, folding it in as you go. Tip the mixture onto a work surface and knead for about 5 minutes, until smooth. Wrap the dough in clingfilm/plastic wrap and chill for at least 30 minutes.

Preheat the oven to 180°C (350°F) Gas 4. Roll out the dough on a lightly floured surface. Use the cookie cutters to stamp out star shapes. Carefully transfer them to the prepared baking sheets. Press together any trimmings and re-roll to make more cookies.

Bake the cookies in the preheated oven for 10–12 minutes, until golden. Transfer them to a wire rack to cool.

Put the icing/confectioner's sugar in a small bowl, add a little lemon juice and stir until smooth. If the icing is too thick, add a drop more lemon juice. Spoon a little icing into the centre of each cookie and spread it out towards the edges using the tip of the spoon. Sprinkle with a few silver balls and leave to set before serving.

225 g/2 sticks unsalted butter, softened

125 g/⅔ cup sugar

1 egg, beaten

1 teaspoon pure vanilla extract

300 g/2⅓ cups plain/all-purpose flour, plus extra for dusting

a pinch of salt

4 tablespoons granulated sugar

yellow, red, green and/or purple food colouring pastes to match your colour scheme

1 tablespoon milk

one flavouring of your choice:

2 tablespoons finely chopped mixed peel; 125 g/4½ oz. chopped glacé cherries; 125 g/4½ oz. chopped pistachios; or 2 tablespoons dried lavender flowers, to match your colour scheme

2 baking sheets, lined with baking parchment

makes about 30

sugared refrigerator cookies

This brightly coloured shortbread will delight both adults and children. They can be easily adapted into a variety of flavours and colours. Match the colour of the sugar to the flavour of the cookies: yellow for lemon, green for pistachio and purple for lavender. Decide on one flavour and corresponding colour scheme before you start.

Cream together the butter and sugar until light and creamy in the bowl of a freestanding mixer (or use an electric whisk and mixing bowl). Add the egg and vanilla and mix well. Sift the flour and salt into the mixture, along with the flavouring you have chosen, and mix again until smooth and the flour is incorporated.

Tip the dough onto a very lightly floured work surface and divide into 2. Roll each piece of dough into a sausage shape roughly 5 cm/2 inches in diameter, wrap tightly in greaseproof/waxed paper and refrigerate until solid – at least 2 hours.

Preheat the oven to 150°C (300°F) Gas 3.

Tip the granulated sugar into a plastic food bag. Using the tip of a wooden skewer, gradually add the colour of food colouring paste you have chosen to match the flavour of the cookie, mixing well until the desired shade is reached. Tip the coloured sugar onto a baking sheet. Remove the cookie dough logs from the fridge and brush them with the milk. Roll in the coloured sugar to coat evenly.

Using a sharp knife, cut the logs into 5-mm/¼-inch slices and arrange on the prepared baking sheets. Bake on the middle shelf of the preheated oven for about 15 minutes, or until pale golden. Leave to cool on the baking sheets for 5 minutes before transferring to a wire rack to cool completely.

drinks for crowds

white sangria

Many people don't realize that sangria can be made with white wine as well as red. This delicious summery version is much lighter and crisper in taste and it's flavour is enhanced by adding seasonal fruits, such as strawberries, to the mix.

1 bottle (750 ml) dry white wine

125 ml/½ cup freshly squeezed orange juice

2 tablespoons sugar

2 oranges, peeled and white pith removed, thinly sliced

1 punnet/pint strawberries, hulled and halved

125 ml/½ cup dry gin

ice cubes, to serve

serves 4–6

Put the white wine, orange juice, sugar, fruit and gin in a large jug/pitcher and refrigerate for 3 hours, until well chilled, stirring often so that the sugar dissolves.

Put the ice cubes in a large serving jug/pitcher and pour over the sangria. Serve immediately.

250 ml/1 cup apple juice

250 ml/1 cup low-sugar lemonade

2 peaches, stoned and roughly chopped

12 strawberries, to garnish

1 bottle (750 ml) Champagne or any sparkling white wine, chilled

ice cubes, to serve

serves 12

summer fruit punch

This recipe is similar to White Wine Sangria only much sweeter with the omission of the gin and inclusion of lemonade. It also has a wonderfully refreshing fizz.

Combine the apple juice, lemonade and peaches in a bowl or large jug/pitcher and refrigerate until chilled.

Put a few scoops of ice cubes in a serving jug/pitcher or glasses with a strawberry to garnish. Add the apple juice mixture and top up with Champagne. Serve immediately.

250 ml/1 cup Pimm's

750 ml/3 cups dry ginger ale

1 tablespoon freshly squeezed lime juice

1 small cucumber, thinly sliced

a handful of fresh mint leaves

serves 4

minty pimm's

This traditional summertime drink is perfect for tennis parties and polo matches. The cucumber is a necessity for serving with Pimm's.

Chill 4 serving glasses. Combine the Pimm's, ginger ale and lime juice in a jug/pitcher. Put the cucmber, mint leaves and ice cubes into the serving glasses and add the Pimm's mixture. Serve immediately.

iced lemon vodka

Try circulating a tray of iced vodka shots at a summer party. The sharp, intensely refreshing flavour goes particularly well with the caviar blinis on page 103.

freshly squeezed juice of 2 lemons plus slices of lemon to serve

175 g/¾ cup sugar

125 ml/½ cup vodka

a resealable bottle or container

8 freezer-frosted shot glasses

serves 8

Put the lemon juice in a jug/pitcher, add the sugar and stir until it has dissolved. Add the vodka, transfer the liquid to the bottle and chill in the freezer. Serve in freezer-frosted shot glasses with small slices of lemon to garnish.

mulled wine

Warm your house and make your guests' hearts glow with this beautiful spicy drink. If you're making it for a big party, add more wine and sugar to the pan as the evening wears on.

2 bottles red wine, 750 ml each

8 whole cloves

2 oranges

3 tablespoons brown sugar

5-cm/2-inch piece fresh ginger, peeled and chopped

1 cinnamon stick

½ teaspoon freshly grated nutmeg

serves 6

Pour the red wine into a medium saucepan. Push the cloves into the oranges, then cut each orange into quarters. Add to the pan, together with the sugar, ginger, cinnamon and nutmeg.

Heat the mixture to simmering point and simmer for about 10 minutes, then serve hot.

mulled cider

For a Christmas gathering, mulled cider makes such a delicious alternative to mulled wine. You could even prepare both and offer your guests a choice of these warming tipples.

500 ml/2 cups traditional dry/hard apple cider

125 ml/1 cup Calvados (French apple brandy) or brandy

750 ml/3 cups cloudy apple juice

75 g/⅓ cup soft dark (or light) brown sugar

thinly pared strip of lemon zest

2 cinnamon sticks

8 cloves

6 evenly sized slices of dried apple, halved, for decoration

serves 10–12

Put the cider, Calvados or brandy, and apple juice in a large saucepan. Add the sugar, lemon zest, cinnamon sticks and cloves and heat very gently until the sugar has dissolved. Heat until almost boiling then turn off the heat, add the halved apple slices and leave in the pan for half an hour for the flavours to infuse. Reheat the punch again, taking care not to boil and serve in heatproof cups or glasses with a slice of the apple in each.

index

recipe credits

Fiona Beckett
grilled pepper, tomato and chilli salad
heirloom tomato, pepper and mozzarella tart
kisir
mini pissaldieres
mulled cider
pea and parma ham crostini
pork and olive empanadas
raspberry and brown sugar meringues
sesame prawn toasts

Julz Beresford
cheese balls
chorizo in red wine
pinchos
spicy Moorish skewers

Susannah Blake
baby rarebits with beetroot and orange relish
blinis with sour cream and caviar
blue cheese and pear crostini
iced lemon vodka
praline and coffee éclairs
sparkly tiara cupcakes
spiced star cookies
strawberry tartlets
white chocolate and cranberry florentines
white chocolate and lemon truffle balls

Maxine Clark
best guacamole with tortilla chips
big pot of cassoulet
dark mushroom and tarragon tart
fillet of beef salad with Thai dressing
Italian chocolate truffles
lasagne al forno
onion, rosemary and roasted garlic tartlets
slow-roasted tomato and herb tartlets with feta
smoked salmon and cucumber sushi rolls
smoked salmon, vodka and sour cream tartlets
spicy crab cups
whole poached salmon with sweet and sour pickled cucumber

Ross Dobson
chilli salt squid
kipfler crisps with sour cream and caviar dip
minty Pimm's
miso and parmesan palmiers
polenta chips with green tabasco mayonnaise
roasted red pepper and walnut dip
smoked trout, celeriac and apple salad
spicy Cajun mixed nuts
summer fruit punch
white sangria

Clare Ferguson
Catalan chickpea salad

Lydia France
anchovy wafers
apple and Calvados pies
black bean chilli in polenta cups with crème fraîche
butternut squash hot shots
Caesar salad tarts
coconut and cardamom chicken
fillet steak on toast with mustard and rocket
flash-seared tuna on rye with horseradish and tarragon cream
grilled lamb skewers with garlic and saffron custard
harissa hoummus with pomegranate vinaigrette
hot crumbed prawns with tomato aioli
lemon buffalo mozzarella and pickled figs on crostini
mini meringues brushed with bitter chocolate
peppered duck, fig and bay skewers
piquant rare duck in chicory boats with crushed peanuts
piri piri mushrooms
prawn cocktail shots
rose marzipan dates
sesame maple turkey fingers
slow roasted tomato galettes with black olive tapenade and goats' cheese
spanish men
spiced pork balls with sticky cider syrup
sticky dates with lemon feta and walnuts
trio of honey-baked camembert with calvados and herbs
twice-marinated salt-lime chicken
vermouth scallops with green olive tapenade
warm spice-rubbed potatoes with rosemary mayonnaise

Jennifer Joyce
crumbled cheese dip with herbs and pomegranate seeds
roasted aubergine and caper dip
swordfish souvlaki bites
warm halloumi bites

Caroline Marson
garlic and herb bread
finger-lickin' drumsticks
fruity coleslaw

Annie Nichols
roasted potato salad

Isidora Popovic
little margherita pizzas with olives
Stilton and celery bites
ginger and chilli caramel cookies

Annie Rigg
cheese straws
sausage rolls
scotch pancakes with smoked salmon
frosted brownie squares
sugared refrigerator cookies

Jennie Shapter
courgette rolls
crab wonton wraps with dipping sauce
halloumi and pepper wraps with salsa verde
mini spring rolls with chilli dipping sauce

Anne Sheasby
mince pies

Fran Warde
artichoke and tomato pastry boats
chicken skewers with sweet chilli
chocolate-dipped strawberries
goat's cheese and pepper crostini
grissini sticks with parma ham
honeyed chicken wings
mulled wine
Parmesan and rosemary wafers
plum pastries
potato skins with green dip
raw vegetable platter
sage and stilton flatbread
smoked oyster and goat's cheese pastries

photography credits

Key: a=above, b=below, r=right, l=left, c=center.

Martin Brigdale
Page 4-5, 37, 47l, 48, 52, 55, 56, 64, 83cr, 98, 102, 155cl, 155cr, 168, 171, 184, 189cr, 194, 198, 205, 213, 214, 218, 221, 225l, 230

Peter Cassidy
Page 9cl, 9cr, 13, 21, 29, 47cl, 47r, 53, 59, 62, 63, 72, 77, 79, 80, 103, 109cr, 109r, 118, 126, 130, 132 inset, 134, 135l, 140, 144, 149 inset, 165 inset, 167, 172, 175, 188, 189l, 189cl, 192 inset, 193 main, 197, 202, 206, 208 inset, 219, 225r, 234, 235 inset

Jean Cazals
Page 1, 2, 3l, 3cl, 3cr, 18, 41, 45, 51, 67, 75, 76, 82, 83l, 83cl, 85, 86, 89, 93, 94, 97, 101, 108, 109cl, 110, 114, 117, 121, 122, 125, 129, 133, 135r, 147, 187, 190, 201, 210

Daniel Farmer
Page 16

Tara Fisher
Pages 138 inset, 227 inset

Richard Jung
Pages 19, 27, 32, 40, 112, 115, 128, 161, 173 inset, 186, 203, 212

Lisa Linder
Pages 38, 105, 135cr, 143, 153, 189r, 217, 228

William Lingwood
Pages 8, 9l, 30, 33, 42, 65, 83r, 90, 232

David Montgomery
Page 231

Diana Miller
Pages 20 inset, 28, 70, 181 inset, 200

David Munns
Page 95 inset

Peter Myers
Page 176

Gloria Nicol
Page 178 inset

William Reavell
Page 57

Debi Treloar
Pages 3r, 14, 46, 47cr, 60, 68, 71, 109l, 113, 139, 148, 152, 156, 180, 209, 224, 233

Ian Wallace
Page 66 inset

Kate Whitaker
Page 3bg, 6-7, 9r, 10-12, 20bg, 22, 23, 25, 26, 31, 34, 35, 36bg, 39, 50, 58, 61, 66bg, 73, 74, 84, 87, 91, 92, 95bg, 96, 100, 104, 116, 119, 127, 132bg, 135cl, 138bg, 141, 146, 149bg, 151, 157, 158, 164, 165bg, 166, 173bg, 174, 178bg, 181bg, 185, 192bg, 195, 196, 208bg, 211, 215, 222, 225cl, 225cr, 226, 227bg, 229, 235bg

Polly Wreford
Pages 136, 155r, 159, 179, 191

Francesca Yorke
Page 36 inset